G000057516

SQL Server Transaction Log Management

By Tony Davis and Gail Shaw

First published by Simple Talk Publishing October 2012

Copyright Tony Davis and Gail Shaw 2012

ISBN: 978-1-906434-96-0

The right of Tony Davis and Gail Shaw to be identified as the authors of this work has been asserted by them in accordance with the Copyright, Designs and Patents Act 1988.

All rights reserved. No part of this publication may be reproduced, stored or introduced into a retrieval system, or transmitted, in any form, or by any means (electronic, mechanical, photocopying, recording or otherwise) without the prior written consent of the publisher. Any person who does any unauthorized act in relation to this publication may be liable to criminal prosecution and civil claims for damages.

This book is sold subject to the condition that it shall not, by way of trade or otherwise, be lent, re-sold, hired out, or otherwise circulated without the publisher's prior consent in any form other than which it is published and without a similar condition including this condition being imposed on the subsequent publisher.

Technical Review and Edit: Kalen Delaney
Additional Material: Jonathan Kehayias and Shawn McGehee
Cover Image by Andy Martin
Typeset by Peter Woodhouse and Gower Associates

Table of Contents

Introduction 11

Chapter 1: Meet the Transaction Log 15

How SQL Server Uses the Transaction Log 15
Write Ahead Logging and Transactional Consistency 16
Transaction Log Backup and Restore 18
Controlling the Size of the Log 20
A Brief Example of Backing up the Transaction Log 22
Summary 26

Chapter 2: Some, But Not Too Much, Log Internals 27

Virtual Log Files and the Active Log 27
Log Truncation and Space Reuse 31
A Peek at How SQL Server Grows the Log 33
Summary 42

Chapter 3: Transaction Logs, Backup and Recovery 43

The Importance of Backups 43
What Backups Do I Need to Take? 45
Database Recovery Models 47
  Choosing the right recovery model 48
  Setting the recovery model 49
  Discovering the recovery model 50
  Switching models 53
Log Backup Logistics 54
  Frequency of log backups 54
  Preserving the log chain 55
  Storing log backups 56
  Automating and verifying backups 57
Summary 58

Chapter 4: Managing the Log in SIMPLE Recovery Model _____ 59

Working in SIMPLE Recovery Model _____ 59

Pros and Cons of SIMPLE Recovery Model _____ 61

Chapter 5: Managing the Log in FULL Recovery Model _____ 63

What Gets Logged? _____ 63

Basics of Log Backup _____ 64

    Are log backups being taken? _____ 64

    How to back up the transaction log _____ 65

    Tail log backups _____ 66

Performing Restore and Recovery _____ 68

    Full restore to point of failure _____ 69

    Restore to end of log backup _____ 72

    Point-in-time restores _____ 77

    Tail log backups when the database is offline _____ 85

Summary _____ 86

Chapter 6: Managing the Log in BULK_LOGGED Recovery Model _____ 89

Minimally Logged Operations _____ 90

Advantages of Minimal Logging and BULK_LOGGED Recovery _____ 98

Implications of Minimally Logged Operations _____ 102

    Crash recovery _____ 103

    Database restores _____ 104

    Log backup size _____ 108

    Tail log backups _____ 109

Best Practices for Use of BULK_LOGGED _____ 115

Summary _____ 117

Chapter 7: Dealing with Excessive Log Growth   119

Sizing and Growing the Log   120

Diagnosing a Runaway Transaction Log   121

    Excessive logging: index maintenance operations   122

    Lack of log space reuse   130

    Other possible causes of log growth   142

Handling a Transaction Log Full Error   146

Mismanagement or What Not To Do   149

    Detach database, delete log file   149

    Forcing log file truncation   150

    Scheduled shrinking of the transaction log   151

Proper Log Management   152

Summary   153

Chapter 8: Optimizing Log Throughput   155

Physical Architecture   155

    You only need one log file   156

    Use a dedicated drive/array for the log file   161

    Use RAID 10 for log drives, if possible   162

Log Fragmentation and Operations that Read the Log   164

    Effect on log backups   167

    Effect on crash recovery   173

Correct Log Sizing   180

What To Do If Things Go Wrong   183

Summary   187

Further Reading   188

Acknowledgements   188

Chapter 9: Monitoring the Transaction Log — 189

Monitoring Tools — 190
Windows Perfmon — 190
Red Gate SQL Monitor — 196

Dynamic Management Views and Functions — 197
Using sys.dm_db_log_space_usage (SQL Server 2012 only) — 198
Using sys.dm_io_virtual_file_stats — 198
Using sys.dm_os_performance_counters — 203

T-SQL and PowerShell Scripting — 204
T-SQL and SSIS — 205
PowerShell — 205

Summary — 210
Further Reading — 210
Acknowledgements — 211

About the Authors

Tony Davis is an Editor with Red Gate Software, based in Cambridge (UK), specializing in databases, and especially SQL Server. He edits articles and writes editorials for both the Simple-talk.com and SQLServerCentral.com websites and newsletters, with a combined audience of over 1.5 million subscribers.

You can sample his short-form written wisdom at either his Simple-Talk.com blog (HTTP://WWW.SIMPLE-TALK.COM/BLOGS/AUTHOR/2130-TONY-DAVIS/) or his SQLServerCentral.com author page (HTTP://WWW.SQLSERVERCENTRAL.COM/AUTHORS/ARTICLES/TONY_DAVIS/295097/). As the editor behind most of the SQL Server-related books published by Red Gate (see HTTP://WWW.SIMPLE-TALK.COM/BOOKS/), he spends much of his time helping others express what they know about SQL Server in as clear and concise a manner as possible. This is his first step into the relative limelight of book authoring. It's been emotional.

Tony was the author of Chapters 1–5, and Chapter 9, co-author of Chapter 8, and contributed some additional material to Chapters 6 and 7.

Gail Shaw is a senior consultant with Xpertease and is based in Johannesburg, South Africa. She specializes in database performance tuning and database recovery, with a particular focus on topics such as indexing strategies, execution plans, and writing T-SQL code that performs well and scales gracefully.

Gail is a Microsoft Certified Master for SQL Server 2008 and a SQL Server MVP. She is a frequent poster on the SQL Server Central forum, writes articles for both SQLServerCentral.com and Simple-Talk.com and blogs on all things relating to database performance on her blog at HTTP://SQLINTHEWILD.CO.ZA. She has spoken at TechEd Africa, the 24 Hours of PASS web event and, on multiple occasions, at the PASS Community summit.

Gail is an Aikido Shodan (1st degree black belt), an avid archer and, in her copious spare time, is pursuing a Master's degree in Computer Science at the University of South Africa.

Gail was the author of Chapters 6 and 7, co-author of Chapter 8, and contributed additional material in various places throughout the book.

About the Technical Reviewer

Kalen Delaney has been working with SQL Server for 25 years, and provides performance consulting services as well as advanced SQL Server training to clients around the world, using her own custom-developed curriculum. She has been a SQL Server MVP since 1993 and has been writing about SQL Server for almost as long. Kalen has spoken at dozens of technical conferences, including every US PASS conference since the organization's founding in 1999.

Kalen is a contributing editor and columnist for SQL Server Magazine and the author or co-author of several of the most deeply technical books on SQL Server, including *SQL Server 2008 Internals* and the upcoming *SQL Server 2012 Internals*, both from Microsoft Press. Kalen blogs at www.SQLBLOG.COM, and her personal website and schedule can be found at www.SQLSERVERINTERNALS.COM.

Acknowledgements

Tony Davis would like to thank:

- **Gail Shaw**. It's been a pleasure to work with Gail on this book. She was tireless in keeping me honest and accurate, and commendably patient in helping me understand some of the finer points of transaction log mechanics.

- **Kalen Delaney**. It was both reassuring and slightly intimidating to have Kalen edit and review my efforts, given how much she knows about this topic, and SQL Server in general. Her efforts have undoubtedly made this a far better book than it would have been otherwise.

- All of the people who give their time to contribute to the SQL Server community knowledge base, in the form of books, articles, blogs and forum posts, as well as technical presentations at events such as SQL Saturday and the PASS Summit. I've worked with many of these people over the years, and learned from all of them.

- **Sarah, my wife**. For her tolerance and patience during the trials and tribulations of writing this book, and for far too many other things to mention here.

Introduction

Associated with every SQL Server database is a primary data file (**.mdf**), possibly some secondary data files (**.ndf**), and a transaction log file (**.ldf**). The purpose of the data files is self-explanatory, but the purpose of the log file remains, for many, shrouded in mystery, and yet it is critical to the everyday operation of SQL Server, and to its ability to recover a database in the event of failure.

A transaction log is a file in which SQL Server stores a record of all the transactions performed on the database with which the log file is associated. In the event of a disaster that causes SQL Server to shut down unexpectedly, such as an instance-level failure or a hardware failure, SQL Server uses the transaction log in order to recover the database to a consistent state, with data integrity intact. Upon restart, a database enters a **crash recovery** process in which the transaction log is read to ensure that all valid, committed data is written to the data files (rolled forward) and the effects of any partial, uncommitted transactions are undone (rolled back). SQL Server also uses the transaction log during normal operation, to identify what it needs to do when a transaction rolls back, due to either an error or a user-specified ROLLBACK statement. In short, the transaction log is the fundamental means by which SQL Server ensures database integrity and the ACID properties of transactions, notably durability.

In addition, backups of the transaction log enable DBAs to restore a database to the state in which it existed at a previous, arbitrary point in time. During the restore phase, SQL Server rolls forward the data changes described in a series of log backup files. We can then recover the database and, via the recovery process described above, SQL Server will ensure that the database is in a transactionally consistent state, at the recovery point.

When a SQL Server database is operating smoothly and performing well, there is no need to be particularly conscious of exactly what the transaction log does, or how it works. As a DBA, you just need to be confident that every database has the correct backup regime in place. When things go wrong, however, a deeper understanding of the transaction log is important for taking corrective action, particularly when a point-in-time restore of a database is urgently required! In this book, we strive to offer just the right level of detail so that every DBA can perform all of the most important duties of a DBA concerning management of the transaction log. This covers performing transaction log backup and restore, monitoring and managing log growth, including quick diagnosis of the causes of rapid growth, and optimizing log architecture to maximize log throughput and availability.

Book Structure

The book starts with a discussion, in Chapters 1 and 2, of how SQL Server uses the transaction log during normal operation as well as during database restore operations and crash recovery. These chapters aim to provide just enough information so that you understand the basic role of the log, how it works, and a little about its internal structure. With this foundation laid, the book sets about describing all of the major necessary management techniques for the transaction log, covering how to:

- **Choose the right recovery model** – SQL Server offers three database recovery models: FULL (the default), SIMPLE, and BULK LOGGED. The DBA must choose the appropriate model according to the business requirements for the database, and then establish maintenance procedures appropriate to that mode. We cover this in Chapter 3, *Transaction Logs, Backup and Recovery*.

- **Perform transaction log backup and restore** – Unless working in SIMPLE model, it is *vital* that the DBA perform regular backups of the transaction log. Once captured in a backup file, the log records can subsequently be applied to a full database backup in order to perform a database restore, and so re-create the database as it existed at a previous point in time, for example, right before a failure. Chapters 4 to 6 cover this in detail, for each of the recovery models.

- **Monitor and manage log growth** – In a busy database, the transaction log can grow rapidly in size. If not regularly backed up, or if inappropriately sized, or assigned incorrect growth characteristics, the transaction log file can fill up, leading to the infamous **"9002" (transaction log full)** error, which puts SQL Server into a "read-only" mode. We deal with this topic in Chapter 7, *Dealing with Excessive Log Growth*.

- **Optimize log throughput and availability** – In addition to basic maintenance such as taking backups, the DBA must take steps to ensure adequate performance of the transaction log. This includes hardware considerations, as well as avoiding situations such as log fragmentation, which can affect the performance of operations that read the log. We cover this topic in Chapter 8, *Optimizing Log Throughput*.

- **Monitor the transaction log** – Having configured hardware for the log array, and pre-sized the log according to workload and maintenance requirements, it's very important that we monitor the I/O performance of the log array, as well as log activity, tracking log growth, log fragmentation, and so on. Chapter 9, *Monitoring the Transaction Log*, covers log monitoring tools and techniques.

Code Examples

You can download every script (denoted Listing X.X) in this book from the following URL: HTTP://WWW.SIMPLE-TALK.COM/REDGATEBOOKS/DAVISSHAW/SQLSERVERTRANSACTIONLOG_CODE.ZIP

Most of the examples use custom-built databases, but a few rely on the readily available `AdventureWorks` database. For SQL Server 2008 and later, you can download it from Microsoft's codeplex site: HTTP://MSFTDBPRODSAMPLES.CODEPLEX.COM/RELEASES/

For SQL Server 2005, use: HTTP://MSFTDBPRODSAMPLES.CODEPLEX.COM/RELEASES/VIEW/4004.

For SQL Server 2005 and 2008, run the file **AdventureWorksDB.msi** (SQL Server 2005) or simply copy the data and log files to your hard drive (SQL Server 2008) and then, in SQL Server Management Studio, attach the files to create the `AdventureWorks` database on your preferred SQL Server instance.

For SQL Server 2008 R2 and later, simply follow the instructions here: HTTP://SOCIAL.TECHNET.MICROSOFT.COM/WIKI/CONTENTS/ARTICLES/3735.SQL-SERVER-SAMPLES-README-EN-US.ASPX#README_FOR_ADVENTURE_WORKS_SAMPLE_DATABASES.

Feedback

We've tried our very best to ensure that this book is useful, technically accurate, and written in plain, simple language. If we've erred on any of these elements, we'd like to hear about it. Please post your feedback and errata to the book page, here:

HTTP://WWW.SIMPLE-TALK.COM/BOOKS/SQL-BOOKS/SQL-SERVER-TRANSACTION-LOG-MANAGEMENT/.

Chapter 1: Meet the Transaction Log

In this chapter, we start with an overview of how SQL Server uses the transaction log, focusing on the Write Ahead Logging mechanism that ensures transactional consistency and durability during normal operation of a SQL Server database. We then offer an initial overview of two of the most significant ways in which it impacts the life of a DBA, namely database restore and recovery, and disk space management.

How SQL Server Uses the Transaction Log

In SQL Server, the transaction log is a physical file, identified conventionally, though not compulsorily, by the extension LDF. SQL Server creates one automatically for any new database, along with the primary data file (commonly identified by the MDF extension), which stores the database objects and the data itself. Generally, each database will have a single transaction log file. It is possible to implement the log as multiple physical files, but SQL Server always writes to the log sequentially; it cannot, and does not, write in parallel to multiple log files and so there is no advantage to having multiple files from the perspective of log throughput. We'll discuss this more in Chapter 8, *Optimizing Log Throughput*, where we'll also explain the exceptional circumstances, such as a full log, where you might have a temporary need for multiple log files.

Whenever T-SQL code makes a change to a database object (DDL), or the data it contains, not only is the data or object updated in the data file, but details of the change are also recorded as a **log record** in the transaction log. Each log record contains the details of a single, specific change made to the database (such as the insert of a single row), so it may require a whole series of log records to describe fully the effects of a single transaction. Certain of these log records will record the ID of the transaction that performed the change, when that transaction started and ended, which pages changed, the data changes that were made, and so on. SQL Server knows how to link these log records together in the right order (more on this in Chapter 2) and so can construct a complete description of the actions of each transaction, which can be performed again as a part of *redo*, or rolled back as a part of *undo*, during a crash recovery operation.

The transaction log is not an audit trail...

The transaction log does not provide an audit trail of changes made to the database; it does not keep a record of the commands executed against the database, just how the data changed as a result.

Write Ahead Logging and Transactional Consistency

Let's consider what happens during a standard multi-row update in SQL Server. Ideally, SQL Server will read the relevant data pages from the data cache, but will first retrieve them from disk if they are not already in the cache. It will acquire all necessary row, page, and table level locks to stabilize the required data, and then begin the data modification transaction. For each target row, it takes an Exclusive lock, and modifies the relevant data page, in memory. It also writes a description of the change to a log record, also in memory, in the log buffer. When all necessary changes are complete, and SQL Server is ready to commit the transaction, it first hardens to disk all of the log records in the buffer, up to the point of the COMMIT. Note that this is not a selective flushing to disk of just the log records relating to the current transaction, but a flushing of all log records up to that point, regardless of whether there are other log records associated with as yet uncommitted transactions.

With all modifications hardened to the physical log file, SQL Server releases all locks and notifies the session that the commit succeeded. At this point, the change is "permanent" and guaranteed to persist through all conditions, including system failure. Note, though, that there has yet to be any mention of SQL Server writing the actual data pages to disk, only the related log records. SQL Server may not write the data pages to disk until later, usually when the next database checkpoint operation occurs.

The Lazy Writer

Another process that scans the data cache, the Lazy Writer, may also write dirty data pages to disk, outside of a checkpoint, if forced to do so by memory pressures.

At each checkpoint, SQL Server scans the data cache and flushes to disk *all* dirty pages in memory. A dirty page is any page in the cache that has changed since SQL Server read it from disk, so that the page in cache is different from what's on disk. Again, this is not a selective flushing; SQL Server flushes out all dirty pages, regardless of whether they contain changes associated with open (uncommitted) transactions. However, the log buffer manager *always guarantees* to write the change descriptions (log records) to the transaction log, on disk, *before* it writes the changed data pages to the physical data files.

This mechanism, termed **write ahead logging**, allows SQL Server to ensure some of the ACID properties (HTTP://MSDN.MICROSOFT.COM/EN-GB/LIBRARY/AA719484(VS.71). ASPX) of database transactions, notably *durability*. By writing changes to the log file first, SQL Server can guarantee that a committed change will persist, even under exceptional circumstances.

For example, let's say a transaction (T1) is committed, and hardened to the log, but SQL Server crashes before a checkpoint occurs. Upon restart, the **crash recovery** process is initiated, which attempts to reconcile the contents of the transactions log file and the data files. It will read the transaction log file and find a series of log records relating to T1 ending with one that confirms the COMMIT. Therefore, it will ensure that all of the operations that comprise transaction T1 are "rolled forward" (redone) so that they are reflected in the data files.

The database checkpoint process

By regularly flushing dirty pages from cache to disk, the database checkpoint process controls the amount of work SQL Server needs to do during crash recovery. If SQL Server had to roll forward the changes for a huge number of committed transactions, then the recovery process could be very lengthy.

Conversely, let's say that T1 starts, a checkpoint occurs, and then, before T1 commits, SQL Server crashes. At the checkpoint, SQL Server would have flushed to disk the dirty pages relating to T1 (along with many others) but the log buffer manager would have ensured that, first, the relevant log records, in cache, were flushed to disk. Since there will be no log record on disk confirming a commit for T1, the crash recovery process will read the relevant operations from the log file, relating to T1, and perform the reverse physical operation on the data, thereby "rolling back" (undoing) the partial effects of an uncommitted transaction.

In this manner, SQL Server can return the database to a consistent state in the event of a crash. More generally, the rollback (undo) process occurs if:

- A ROLLBACK command is issued for an explicit transaction.

- An error occurs and XACT_ABORT is turned on.

- If the database detects that communication has been broken between the database and the client that instigated the transactions.

In such circumstances, the log records pertaining to an interrupted transaction, or one for which the ROLLBACK command is explicitly issued, are read and the changes rolled back. In these ways, SQL Server ensures transaction atomicity, i.e. that either all the actions associated with a transaction succeed as a unit, or that they all fail. As such, the transaction log represents one of the fundamental means by which SQL Server ensures data consistency and integrity during normal day-to-day operation.

Transaction Log Backup and Restore

The transaction log plays another vital role in that it provides the mechanism by which we can restore a database to a previous point in time, in the event of a disaster. With proper planning and management, we can use backups of these log files to restore our database to the state it existed just before it became corrupted or unusable.

As discussed earlier, a transaction log contains a series of log records, each one describing a single database action, stored sequentially according to when that action occurred in the database. For a given transaction, first a log record will be recorded signifying the start of the transaction, then a series of log records describing each action performed, and finally a record for the transaction commit. It's a mistake, however, to think of the log records for each transaction being stored neatly together; they will be interspersed with records relating to the actions of many other transactions occurring at around the same time.

When operating a database in FULL or BULK_LOGGED recovery model (we cover recovery models in more detail in Chapter 3), it is possible to take log backups. These log backups write into a backup file all the log records that have been entered since the last log backup or, if this is the first-ever log backup, since the first full database backup. If the log chain (discussed in Chapter 3) is broken, then the first log backup we take after this event will capture all records added to the log since the first full or differential backup taken after the chain was broken.

During a restore operation, we can then restore the most recent full database backup, followed by the complete chain of log backup files up to the one that covers the point in time to which we wish to restore the database. If we restore completely the last log backup file in the chain, then the recovery process will return the database to the state consistent with the time of the last committed transaction in that backup file. Alternatively, we can stop the restore process at a specific point in time within the final log backup, and then the database recovery process will return the database to a consistent state for that time. We'll discuss these operations in much more detail in Chapter 5.

For reasons that will become clearer as we progress, and which we discuss in detail in Chapter 4, it is not possible to take log backups for databases operating in SIMPLE recovery model, and so any database restore operations for such databases must reply solely on full (and differential) database backups.

Controlling the Size of the Log

Implicit in the idea that we can take log backups for use in database restore operations, is the notion that, at least until a log backup occurs, the transaction log must retain every single log record since the last log backup (or first-ever full backup if there has never been a log backup). If SQL Server allowed any of the existing log records to be overwritten by new log records, then the subsequent log backup would contain an incomplete description of all the actions performed on the database since the last log backup, and it would be unusable in any restore operation.

Internally, SQL Server organizes the transaction log into multiple sections, called Virtual Log Files (VLFs), and a VLF is the smallest unit of "space reuse" (a.k.a. **truncation**) in the log. If a VLF contains even a single log record that has yet to be included in a log backup, then that VLF is "active" and SQL Server can't reuse any space within that VLF. In fact, there are several other reasons why a VLF might remain active, even after all its log records are included in a backup; for example, if it contains log records relating to an open (uncommitted) transaction. However, we'll discuss that in much more detail in Chapter 2.

The important point to note for now is that for a FULL or BULK_LOGGED recovery model database, a log backup is the *only* action that can truncate the log, i.e. enable reuse of space within the transaction log. As such, the transaction log will hold a full and complete record of the transactions performed since the last transaction log backup. SQL Server logs all operations in these recovery models, writing log records that describe every single action performed by every single transaction that modifies data or objects in a SQL Server database, and so the log file can grow very large, very quickly, in busy systems.

Truncation and the size of the transaction log

A common misconception is that truncating the log file deletes log records and the file reduces in size. It does not; truncation of a log file is merely the act of marking space as available for reuse. We discuss truncation, in the context of each of the different recovery models, in more detail in subsequent chapters.

Therefore, when working in FULL and BULK LOGGED recovery models, **it is vital** that you perform **regular transaction log backups**, in addition to full backups and, optionally, differential backups. Many novice or part-time DBAs perform full backups on their databases, but they don't perform transaction log backups. As a result, the transaction log is not truncated, and it grows and grows until the drive it is on runs out of disk space, causing SQL Server to enter read-only mode.

When a log backup occurs, any VLF that is no longer active becomes eligible for truncation, meaning simply that SQL Server can reuse its space to store new log records. Truncation of the log will occur as soon as the log backup is taken, assuming no other factors, such as an in-progress database backup operation, are delaying truncation. We'll cover some of the other factors that may delay truncation of VLFs even after log backup, as well as factors that keep large swathes of the log active that otherwise wouldn't need to be, such as a rogue, long-running uncommitted transaction, or database mirroring, or replication processes, in Chapter 7.

COPY_ONLY *backups of the transaction log*

An exception to the rule of log backups truncating the log is the COPY_ONLY log backup. A COPY_ONLY log backup exists "independently" of the normal log backup scheme; it does not break the log backup chain.

In a SIMPLE recovery model database, by contrast, log truncation can occur immediately upon checkpoint. SQL Server flushes cached dirty pages to disk (after first writing the transaction details) and then immediately truncates any VLFs that are no longer active, so that the space can store new log records. This also explains why log backups are meaningless for SIMPLE recovery model databases.

A Brief Example of Backing up the Transaction Log

In order to illustrate some of the concepts we've discussed in this first chapter, we'll walk through a very simple example of backing up the transaction log for a database operating in FULL recovery model. We'll save the full details of the individual processes and commands to later chapters.

Data and backup file locations

Rather than use the default location for the data and log file (C:\Program Files\Microsoft SQL Server\MSSQL10.MSSQLSERVER\MSSQL\Data), the examples in this chapter assume that they are located in D:\SQLData, and that all backups are located in D:\SQLBackups. When running the examples, simply modify these locations as appropriate for your system (and note that in a real system, we wouldn't store everything on the same drive!).

In Listing 1.1, we create a new TestDB database on a SQL Server 2008 instance, and then immediately obtain the size of the log file using the DBCC SQLPERF (LOGSPACE) command.

```
USE master ;

IF DB_ID('TestDB') IS NOT NULL
    DROP DATABASE TestDB ;

CREATE DATABASE TestDB ON
(
  NAME = TestDB_dat,
  FILENAME = 'D:\SQLData\TestDB.mdf'
) LOG ON
(
  NAME = TestDB_log,
  FILENAME = 'D:\SQLData\TestDB.ldf'
) ;

DBCC SQLPERF(LOGSPACE) ;
```

	Database Name	Log Size (MB)	Log Space Used (%)	Status
32	Test	5.679688	92.52923	0
33	TestDB	0.9921875	29.6752	0
34	SimpleRecovery	563.4922	1.639643	0

Listing 1.1: Initial log file size for the new `TestDB` database.

As you can see, the log file is currently about 1 MB in size, and about 30% full.

The model *database*

The properties of the `model` *database determine the initial size and growth characteristics of new user databases on an instance, as well as the default recovery model that each database will adopt (*`FULL`*, in this case). We'll discuss the impact of these properties in more detail in Chapter 8.*

We can confirm the size of the file simply by locating the physical files on disk, as shown in Figure 1.1.

TestDB.mdf   2,240 KB   SQL Server Database Primary Data File
TestDB.ldf   1,024 KB   SQL Server Database Transaction Log File

Figure 1.1: Data and log file for `TestDB`.

Let's now perform a full database backup (i.e. backing up the data file) for `TestDB`, as shown in Listing 1.2 (you'll first need to create the `SQLBackups` directory). Note that this backup operation ensures the database truly is operating in `FULL` recovery model; more on this in Chapter 3.

```
-- full backup of the database
BACKUP DATABASE TestDB
TO DISK ='D:\SQLBackups\TestDB.bak'
WITH INIT;
GO
```

Listing 1.2: Initial full database backup of `TestDB`.

There is no change in the size of the data or log file as a result of this backup operation, or in the percentage of log space used, which is perhaps unsurprising given that there are no user tables or data in the database as yet. Let's put that right, and create a table called LogTest on this database, fill it with a million rows of data, and recheck the log file size, as shown in Listing 1.3. Jeff Moden, the author of this script, is seen regularly on the SQLServerCentral.com forums (HTTP://WWW.SQLSERVERCENTRAL.COM/FORUMS/), and we reproduce it here with his kind permission. Do not worry about the details of the code (we use it several times throughout the book); the only important thing here is that it's a highly efficient way to insert many rows. Still, this code may take several seconds to execute on your machine, due to all the work going on behind the scenes, writing to, and growing, the data and log files.

```
USE TestDB ;
GO
IF OBJECT_ID('dbo.LogTest', 'U') IS NOT NULL
    DROP TABLE dbo.LogTest ;
--====== AUTHOR: Jeff Moden
--====== Create and populate 1,000,000 row test table.
-- "SomeID" has range of 1 to 1000000 unique numbers
-- "SomeInt" has range of 1 to 50000 non-unique numbers
-- "SomeLetters2";"AA"-"ZZ" non-unique 2-char strings
-- "SomeMoney"; 0.0000 to 99.9999 non-unique numbers
-- "SomeDate" ; >=01/01/2000 and <01/01/2010 non-unique
-- "SomeHex12"; 12 random hex characters (ie, 0-9,A-F)
SELECT TOP 1000000
        SomeID = IDENTITY( INT,1,1 ),
        SomeInt = ABS(CHECKSUM(NEWID())) % 50000 + 1 ,
        SomeLetters2 = CHAR(ABS(CHECKSUM(NEWID())) % 26 + 65)
          + CHAR(ABS(CHECKSUM(NEWID())) % 26 + 65) ,
        SomeMoney = CAST(ABS(CHECKSUM(NEWID())) % 10000 / 100.0 AS MONEY) ,
        SomeDate = CAST(RAND(CHECKSUM(NEWID())) * 3653.0 + 36524.0
                                                AS DATETIME) ,
        SomeHex12 = RIGHT(NEWID(), 12)
INTO    dbo.LogTest
FROM    sys.all_columns ac1
        CROSS JOIN sys.all_columns ac2 ;

DBCC SQLPERF(LOGSPACE) ;
```

	Database Name	Log Size (MB)	Log Space Used (%)	Status
32	Test	5.679688	92.52923	0
33	TestDB	99.74219	93.22765	0
34	SimpleRecovery	563.4922	1.639643	0

Listing 1.3: Inserting a million rows into the `LogTest` table, in `TestDB`.

Notice that the log file size has ballooned to almost 100 MB and the log is 93% full (the figures might be slightly different on your system). If we were to insert more data, it would have to grow in size to accommodate more log records. Again, we can confirm the size increases from the physical files (the data file has grown to 64 MB).

We can perform another full database backup at this point, by rerunning Listing 1.2, and it will make no difference to the size of the log file, or the percentage of space used in the file. Instead, however, let's back up the transaction log file and recheck the values, as shown in Listing 1.4.

```
-- now back up the transaction log
BACKUP Log TestDB
TO DISK ='D:\SQLBackups\TestDB_log.trn'
WITH INIT;
GO

DBCC SQLPERF(LOGSPACE) ;
```

	Database Name	Log Size (MB)	Log Space Used (%)	Status
32	Test	5.679688	92.52923	0
33	TestDB	99.74219	6.309724	0
34	SimpleRecovery	563.4922	1.639643	0

Listing 1.4: Backing up the transaction log for `TestDB`.

The log file is still the same physical size but, by backing up the file, SQL Server is able to truncate the log, making space in the inactive VLFs in the log file available for reuse; it can write new log records without needing to grow the log file. In addition, of course, we've captured the log records into a backup file and can use that backup file as part of the database recovery process, should we need to restore the `TestDB` database to a previous state.

Summary

In this first chapter, we've introduced the transaction log, and explained how SQL Server uses it to maintain data consistency and integrity, via a write ahead logging mechanism. We've also described, and briefly demonstrated, how a DBA can capture the contents of the transaction log file into a backup file, for use as part of a database recovery operation. Finally, we stressed the importance of backups in controlling the size of the transaction log.

In the next chapter, we'll take a closer look at the architecture of the transaction log.

Chapter 2: Some, But Not Too Much, Log Internals

Much as we would like to avoid it, some discussion of the internal structure of the transaction log, and the internal processes that work on it, is very helpful in understanding the appropriate log maintenance techniques, and in troubleshooting log-related problems. Others have tackled this topic before. The article, *Understanding Logging and Recovery in SQL Server* (HTTP://TECHNET.MICROSOFT.COM/EN-US/MAGAZINE/2009.02.LOGGING.ASPX) by Paul Randal, and the book, *Microsoft SQL Server 2008 Internals* by Kalen Delaney, are two very good examples, so we will keep things brief here.

Virtual Log Files and the Active Log

As discussed briefly in Chapter 1, internally, SQL Server divides a transaction log file into a number of sections called **Virtual Log Files** (VLFs). Figure 2.1 depicts a transaction log for a newly created database, composed of four empty VLFs.

Figure 2.1:   A transaction log with four empty VLFs.

Transaction log files are **sequential** files; in other words, SQL Server writes to the transaction log sequentially (unlike data files, which SQL Server writes in a more random fashion, as applications modify data in random data pages).

Storage considerations

The different manner in which SQL Server writes to the data and log files means that they also have different storage considerations, for example in regard to the appropriate RAID configuration for the disk drives that store each type of file. We discuss this in more detail in Chapter 8.

SQL Server stamps each log record inserted into the log file with a **Logical Sequence Number (LSN)**. When we create a new database, with its associated log file, the first log record marks the logical start of the log file, which at this stage will coincide with the start of the physical file. The LSNs are then ever increasing, so a log record with an LSN of 5 records an action that occurred immediately before the one with an LSN of 6. The most recent log record will always have the highest LSN, and marks the end of the logical file (discussed in more detail shortly).

Log records associated with a given transaction are linked in an **LSN chain**. Specifically, log records are "backwards chained;" each log record stores the sequence number of the log record that preceded it in a particular transaction. This enables SQL Server to perform rollback, undoing each log record in exact reverse order.

An important concept is that of the "active log." The start of the active log is the "*oldest log record that is required for a successful database-wide rollback or by another activity or operation in the database.*" The LSN of this log record is MinLSN. In other words, the MinLSN is the LSN of the log record relating to the oldest open transaction, or to one that is still required by some other database operation or activity. The log record with the highest LSN (i.e. the most recent record added) marks the end of the active log. SQL Server writes all subsequent records to the logical end of the log.

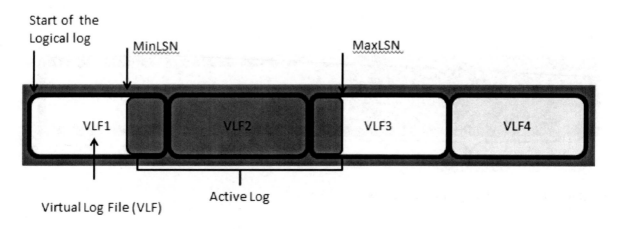

Figure 2.2:   A transaction log showing the active portion of the log.

Note that you may occasionally hear the MinLSN referred to as the **tail** of the log, and MaxLSN as the **head** of the log. A VLF that contains any part of the active log is active; a VLF that contains no part of the active log is inactive. In Figure 2.2, VLFs 1 to 3 are all active. In short, a log record is no longer part of the active log if it is older (i.e. has a lower LSN) than the MinLSN record and this will be true only if the following two conditions are met:

1. No other database process, including a transaction log backup when using FULL or BULK LOGGED recovery models, requires it to remain in the active log.

2. It relates to a transaction that is committed, and so is no longer required for rollback.

For example, consider a case where the MinLSN is a log record for an open transaction (T1) that started at 9.00 a.m. and takes 30 minutes to run. A subsequent transaction (T2) starts at 9.10 a.m. and finishes at 9.11 a.m.. Figure 2.3 shows a very simplified depiction of this situation (our VLFs hold only four log records!).

Figure 2.3: VLFs filling with log records.

VLF2 contains no log records relating to open transactions, but all these log records remain part of the active log since they all have LSNs greater than `MinLSN`. In Figure 2.4, the action has moved on. A third transaction (T3) has started, and T1 has completed its final update, and committed.

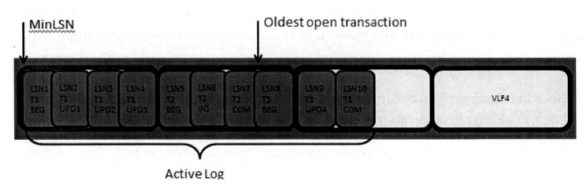

Figure 2.4: Until a log backup, the tail of the log is "pinned."

Now, the log record for the oldest open transaction is LSN8, but the `MinLSN` is still LSN1, and so VLFs 1–3 are all active. Why? Our database is operating in the `FULL` recovery model and until the next log backup operation, all of these log records must remain in the active log. In other words, LSN1 is the oldest log record still required by another database process or activity, in this case a log backup.

Log Truncation and Space Reuse

A very important point to remember is that the smallest unit of truncation in the log file is not the individual log record or log block, but the VLF. If there is just one log record in a VLF that is still part of the active log, then the VLF is active and SQL Server cannot reuse space in that VLF.

Log truncation is the act of marking a VLF as inactive. Generally, for a FULL or BULK_LOGGED recovery model database, once we've captured in a log backup all of the log records in a VLF, then that VLF is marked inactive, assuming that no other process requires those records to remain in the active log.

In Figure 2.5, a log backup directly follows the commit of T1. In this case, VLF1 will no longer hold any part of the active log and SQL Server can truncate it. Both VLF2 and VLF3 are still active. VLF4 is still unused.

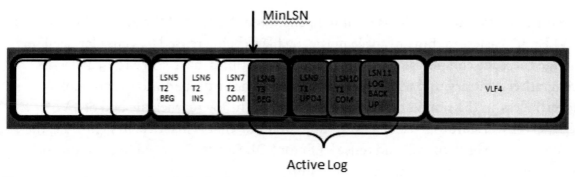

Figure 2.5:   Log truncation via log backup.

In this manner, as transactions start and are committed, we can imagine (somewhat simplistically) the tail and head of the log moving left to right across Figure 2.5, so that VLFs that previously contained part of the active log now become inactive (VLF1), and VLFs that were previously untouched will become part of the active log (VLF4). In a SIMPLE recovery model database, we would get the same situation as depicted in Figure 2.5, if we replaced the log backup with a checkpoint operation.

It's important to remember that even after a checkpoint (for SIMPLE recovery) or a log backup (for FULL or BULK_LOGGED recovery) a VLF may still not be eligible for truncation if it contains log records that must remain part of the active log for other reasons. For example, it may be that these log records relate to an open transaction and so SQL Server requires them for possible rollback. If, in Figure 2.5, we swap the positions of the log records for the T1 commit and the log backup, then VLF1 would not be eligible for truncation, despite the log backup, since the MinLSN would be "pinned" at LSN1 until T1 committed.

Alternatively, these records may still be required because some other database operation, such as database mirroring or replication or CDC (Change Data Capture) has yet to process them.

In either case, the VLFs containing these log records will remain active, despite the log backup or checkpoint. A later log backup will mark these VLFs as inactive, assuming that, by that point, they no longer contain any part of the active log.

The final question to consider is what happens when the head of the log reaches the end of VLF4. It's easiest to think of space in the log file as being reused in a circular fashion, though there are complicating factors that can sometimes make space reuse patterns seem rather arbitrary, and which we're not going to delve deeper into in this book. Nevertheless, in the simplest case, once the head of the log reaches the end of a VLF, SQL Server will start to reuse the next sequential VLF that is inactive. In Figure 2.5, the head will "wrap back round" and reuse VLF1 (or SQL Server may need to grow the log, depending on how much extra space it requires).

If no further VLFs were available at all, the log would need to auto-grow and add more VLFs. If this is not possible, because auto-growth is disabled, or the disk housing the log file is full, then the logical end of the active log will meet the physical end of the log file, the transaction log is full, and SQL Server will issue the 9002 "transaction log full" error and the database will become read-only.

This architecture explains the reason why a very long-running transaction, or a replicated transaction that fails to dispatch to the distribution database, or a disconnected mirror, among others, can cause the log to grow very large. For example, in Figure 2.5, we can imagine what happens if T1 does not commit. Other transactions start and eventually VLF 4 is full and there aren't any inactive VLFs. Even if every transaction that started after MinLSN has committed, SQL Server can reuse none of the space in these VLFs, as all the VLFs are still part of the active log.

You can see this in action quite easily if you return to our example from Chapter 1. First, rerun Listing 1.1 to drop and re-create the TestDB database. Then create a small sample table, update one of the rows in the table within an explicit transaction, and leave the transaction open (do not COMMIT it). In a second tab within SSMS, run the scripts in Listings 1.2 to 1.4. This time you should see that the log backup does *not* make space available for reuse. However, if you then commit the transaction and rerun the log backup, SQL Server reuses the space.

In such cases, where the "area" occupied by the active log is very large, with a lot of space that is not reusable, at some point, the log file will have to grow in size (and grow, and grow…). We'll discuss other factors that delay the truncation of the log file in Chapter 7.

A Peek at How SQL Server Grows the Log

SQL Server decides the optimum size and number of VLFs to allocate. It will allocate a certain number based on the initial size of the log, and it will add a certain additional number of VLFs each time the log auto-grows, based on the size of the auto-growth increment.

Let's re-create our TestDB database from Chapter 1, but this time exerting some control over the log file size and auto-growth (rather than just accepting the defaults from model, as we did before). In Listing 2.1, we create a database with a small log file (2 MB)

and allow it to grow in small, fixed increments of 16 MB (settings based on those for
AdventureWorks2008). We set the database to FULL recovery model, create in it a
table, PrimaryTable_Large, perform a full database backup and, finally, check the
log space use.

```
USE master ;

IF DB_ID('TestDB') IS NOT NULL
    DROP DATABASE TestDB ;

CREATE DATABASE TestDB ON PRIMARY
  (   NAME = N'TestDB'
    , FILENAME = N'D:\SQLData\TestDB.mdf'
    , SIZE = 199680KB
    , FILEGROWTH = 16384KB
  )
  LOG ON
  (   NAME = N'TestDB_log'
    , FILENAME = N'D:\SQLData\TestDB_log.ldf'
    , SIZE = 2048KB
    , FILEGROWTH = 16384KB
  );
GO


USE TestDB
Go
IF OBJECT_ID('dbo.PrimaryTable_Large', 'U') IS NOT NULL
    DROP TABLE dbo.PrimaryTable_Large
GO
CREATE TABLE PrimaryTable_Large
    (
      ID INT IDENTITY
            PRIMARY KEY ,
      SomeColumn CHAR(4) NULL ,
      Filler CHAR(1500) DEFAULT ''
    );
GO

ALTER DATABASE TestDB SET RECOVERY FULL;
```

```
/*Initial full database backup of TestDB*/
BACKUP DATABASE TestDB
TO DISK ='D:\SQLBackups\TestDB.bak'
WITH INIT;
GO


DBCC SQLPERF(LOGSPACE) ;
/*Log Size (MB): 2, Log Space used (%): 18*/
```

Listing 2.1:   Re-creating the TestDB database, plus PrimaryTable_Large.

We can interrogate the VLF architecture using a command called **DBCC LogInfo**, as shown in Listing 2.2.

Interrogating VLFs using DBCC LogInfo

DBCC LogInfo *is an undocumented and unsupported command – at least there is very little written about it by Microsoft. We'll use it in this chapter to peek at the VLFs, but we won't go into detail about all the information it returns.*

```
-- how many VLFs?
USE TestDB;
GO
DBCC Loginfo
GO
```

	FileId	FileSize	StartOffset	FSeqNo	Status	Parity	CreateLSN
1	2	458752	8192	30	2	64	0
2	2	458752	466944	0	0	0	0
3	2	458752	925696	0	0	0	0
4	2	712704	1384448	0	0	0	0

Listing 2.2:   Four VLFs in the newly created TestDB database.

Note that four rows are returned, meaning that we have four VLFs. We are not too concerned right now with the meaning of the columns returned, but we'll note the following:

- The initial log size was 2 MB, and three of the four VLFs are just under 0.5 MB in size, and one is over, as seen in the `FileSize` column (in Bytes).

- A `Status` value of 2 indicates an active VLF that cannot be overwritten, and a value of 0 indicates an inactive VLF where space can be reused. Currently, we have one active VLF.

- The `FSeqNo` (first sequence number) column indicates the logical order of the VLFs in the log. Our single active VLF is logically the first VLF (the value starts at one more than the highest `FSeqNo` in the model database, as explained by Paul Randal, HTTP://WWW.SQLSKILLS.COM/BLOGS/PAUL/POST/INITIAL-VLF-SEQUENCE-NUMBERS-AND-DEFAULT-LOG-FILE-SIZE.ASPX).

- The `CreateLSN` is the LSN of the auto-growth event, or `ALTER DATABASE` operation, which grew the log and so created the VLF. Zero indicates that these VLFs were created when the database was created.

Let's now add 1,500 rows to our table, recheck log space use, and re-interrogate `DBCC LogInfo`.

```
USE TestDB;
GO
INSERT  INTO PrimaryTable_Large
        ( SomeColumn, Filler
        )
        SELECT TOP 1500
                'abcd ',
                REPLICATE('a', 200)
        FROM    msdb.sys.columns a
                CROSS JOIN msdb.sys.columns b
GO

DBCC SQLPERF(LOGSPACE) ;


/*Log Size: 18 MB ; Log Space Used: 16%*/

DBCC Loginfo
GO
```

	FileId	FileSize	StartOffset	FSeqNo	Status	Parity	CreateLSN
1	2	458752	8192	30	2	64	0
2	2	458752	466944	31	2	64	0
3	2	458752	925696	32	2	64	0
4	2	712704	1384448	33	2	64	0
5	2	4194304	2097152	34	2	64	33000000037600057
6	2	4194304	6291456	0	0	0	33000000037600057
7	2	4194304	10485760	0	0	0	33000000037600057
8	2	4194304	14680064	0	0	0	33000000037600057

Listing 2.3: VLFs after adding 1,500 rows.

Having inserted only 1,500 rows, the log has already auto-grown. We see four new VLFs (note that the CreateLSN values are non-zero, and the same in each case, because SQL Server created them in a single auto-grow event). The auto-growth increment was 16 MB and each new VLF is roughly 4 MB in size. The first of the new VLFs (FSeqNo 34) is active, but the rest are yet unused. The log is now 18 MB, as expected, and is 16% full.

Let's now perform a log backup and recheck our stats.

```
/*now a log backup*/
BACKUP Log TestDB
TO DISK ='D:\SQLBackups\TestDB_log.bak'
WITH INIT;
GO

DBCC SQLPERF(LOGSPACE) ;
/*Log Size: 18 MB ; Log Space Used: 6%*/

-- how many VLFs?
USE TestDB;
GO
DBCC Loginfo
GO
```

	FileId	FileSize	StartOffset	FSeqNo	Status	Parity	CreateLSN
1	2	458752	8192	30	0	64	0
2	2	458752	466944	31	0	64	0
3	2	458752	925696	32	0	64	0
4	2	712704	1384448	33	0	64	0
5	2	4194304	2097152	34	2	64	33000000037600057
6	2	4194304	6291456	0	0	0	33000000037600057
7	2	4194304	10485760	0	0	0	33000000037600057
8	2	4194304	14680064	0	0	0	33000000037600057

Listing 2.4:   VLF usage after log backup.

Thanks to the log backup, the log is now only 6% full. The first four VLFs are truncated, and so are available for reuse. Let's grow the log a second time, adding 15K rows (simply rerun Listing 2.3 and adjust the number of rows).

	FileId	FileSize	StartOffset	FSeqNo	Status	Parity	CreateLSN
1	2	458752	8192	30	0	64	0
2	2	458752	466944	31	0	64	0
3	2	458752	925696	32	0	64	0
4	2	712704	1384448	33	0	64	0
5	2	4194304	2097152	34	2	64	33000000037600057
6	2	4194304	6291456	35	2	64	33000000037600057
7	2	4194304	10485760	36	2	64	33000000037600057
8	2	4194304	14680064	37	2	64	33000000037600057
9	2	4194304	18874368	38	2	64	37000000516200030
10	2	4194304	23068672	39	2	64	37000000516200030
11	2	4194304	27262976	40	2	64	37000000516200030
12	2	4194304	31457280	0	0	0	37000000516200030

Figure 2.6:   VLFs after the second load, of 15K rows.

SQL Server fills VLFS 34–37 (arising from the previous auto-growth). The original four VLFs (30–33) are available for reuse, but SQL Server opts to grow the log immediately, rather than reuse them first, and then starts filling the first three of the new VLFs (38–40).

In this case, SQL Server grows the log simply because if it had used the original four small VLFs it would not have had the required **log reservation** space necessary in the event that it needed to roll back the transaction.

The process of rolling back a transaction requires a series of operations that will undo the effects of that transaction. These **compensating operations** generate log records, just as does any other database change. Log reservation is the amount of log space (per transaction) that SQL Server must keep free in order to accommodate these compensation log records.

Accordingly, big transactions that write many records will also need quite a large log reservation. SQL Server releases this additional space once a transaction commits. Chapter 7 (Listing 7.1) provides a query that will display log bytes written and reserved by a transaction. If we had run the 15K-row insert inside an explicit transaction, without committing it, and in another session had run Listing 7.1 to find out how much log space SQL Server reserved for this transaction, we'd have seen it was about 5.3 MB. The total space in those first four VLFs is only 2 MB, which is insufficient to store the compensation operations that may be necessary, and so SQL Server grows the log immediately. In the absence of any log reservation calculation, SQL Server would simply have filled the available VLFs and then grown the log.

As such, the exact growth behavior depends very much on the patterns of user activity, and the size of the transactions. If we replace the 15K row insert with a series of three, smaller inserts (1,500 rows, 5,000, rows, 3,500 rows, for example) then we see something like Figure 2.7.

	FileId	FileSize	StartOffset	FSeqNo	Status	Parity	CreateLSN
1	2	458752	8192	38	2	128	0
2	2	458752	466944	39	2	128	0
3	2	458752	925696	32	0	64	0
4	2	712704	1384448	33	0	64	0
5	2	4194304	2097152	34	2	64	33000000037600057
6	2	4194304	6291456	35	2	64	33000000037600057
7	2	4194304	10485760	36	2	64	33000000037600057
8	2	4194304	14680064	37	2	64	33000000037600057
9	2	4194304	18874368	40	2	64	39000000037400121
10	2	4194304	23068672	0	0	0	39000000037400121
11	2	4194304	27262976	0	0	0	39000000037400121
12	2	4194304	31457280	0	0	0	39000000037400121

Figure 2.7:   VLFs after three smaller data loads.

Notice that SQL Server fills the VLFs added by the first auto-growth (34–37), and then cycles back to the start and uses the first two of the original VLFs (now reused as 38 and 39). This happens because, here, these VLFs will accommodate the log reservation required by the smaller initial inserts. SQL Server then grows the log again and starts to use the first of these (40) rather the remaining two original VLFs.

We hope that this provides a little insight into how SQL Server auto-grows the log. Of course, in these examples, we've been adding a relatively small number of rows. As a final test, rerun Listing 2.1, followed by Listing 2.3, but this time add 1 million rows. The log will now be about 2.1 GB in size and about 80% full. Figure 2.8 shows the output of DBCC LogInfo.

	FileId	FileSize	StartOffset	FSeqNo	Status	Parity	CreateLSN
432	2	4194304	1793064...	461	2	64	378000000396300...
433	2	4194304	1797259...	462	2	64	381000000599700...
434	2	4194304	1801453...	463	2	64	381000000599700...
435	2	4194304	1805647...	464	2	64	381000000599700...
436	2	4194304	1809842...	465	2	64	381000000599700...
437	2	4194304	1814036...	0	0	0	384000000815400...
438	2	4194304	1818230...	0	0	0	384000000815400...
439	2	4194304	1822425...	0	0	0	384000000815400...
440	2	4194304	1826619...	0	0	0	384000000815400...
441	2	4194304	1830813...	0	0	0	388000000204800...
442	2	4194304	1835008.	0	0	0	388000000204800...
443	2	4194304	1839202...	0	0	0	388000000204800...
444	2	4194304	1843396...	0	0	0	388000000204800...

Query executed successfully.   tonytest.testnet (10.0 SP1) | RED-GATE\tony.davis (51) | TestDB | 00:00:00 | 536 rows

Figure 2.8: The output of DBCC LogInfo after adding 1 million rows.

Now we have 536 VLFs (436 of which are in use). Note that it may seem as if SQL Server has "overgrown" the log, but again we must factor in log reservation requirements. In this case, SQL Server had to add considerable extra space in case it needed to roll back the insert.

A transaction log that auto-grows frequently, in small increments, will have a very large number of small VLFs. This phenomenon is **log fragmentation**. Essentially, the initial size and relatively small growth increments we've chosen for this database are inappropriate for this sort of data load and lead to the creation of a large number of VLFs.

It's possible that log file fragmentation can degrade the performance of SQL Server processes that need to read the log, such as crash recovery and log backups. We will discuss this in more detail in Chapter 8, and show how to avoid fragmentation by correctly sizing and growing the log file.

Summary

This chapter provides minimal background information regarding the architecture of the transaction log; hopefully, just enough so that you can understand the basic issues and potential problems relating to truncation, space reuse, and fragmentation, in the log file.

In Chapter 3, we move on to a more detailed discussion of the role of the transaction log in database restore and recovery.

Chapter 3: Transaction Logs, Backup and Recovery

Unless your database is operating in SIMPLE recovery model, it is very important that you take regular log backups. This will control the size of the transaction log, and ensure that, in the event of a disaster, you are able to restore your database to some point shortly before the disaster occurred. These transaction log backups will be performed alongside regular full database (data file) backups, and possibly differential database backups.

If you're backing up a test system where you don't need to restore to a previous point in time, or it's clear from the Service Level Agreement (SLA) that you can meet database recovery requirements simply by restoring the most recent full (plus differential) backups, then you should probably operate the database in `SIMPLE` recovery model. If you need more fine-grained control over the point at which you can recover a database, then `FULL` recovery model is the right choice. Let's discuss these issues in more detail.

The Importance of Backups

Consider a situation in which a SQL Server database crashes, perhaps due to a catastrophic hardware failure, and the data files (`mdf`, plus any `ndf` files), along with the transaction log file (`ldf` file), are no longer accessible.

In the worst case, if no backups (copies) of these files exist elsewhere, then you will suffer 100% data loss. In order to ensure that you can recover the database and its data as it existed at some point before the server crashed, or before data was lost or corrupted for other reasons, the DBA needs to make regular backups of both the data and log files.

A DBA can perform three main types of backup (although only the first two apply for a database in the SIMPLE recovery model).

- **Full database backup** – A copy of the data files. Essentially, this provides a complete archive of your database as it existed at the time the backup operation *finished* (the backup will include the effects of any transaction that completed before the data-copying portion of the backup was finished. Any transactions that are still open when SQL Server starts backing up the necessary portion of the transaction log are not included). A full backup includes all user objects and data as well as relevant system information.

- **Differential database backup** – A copy of any changes made to the database since the last full backup. There is an inextricable link between a differential backup and the most recent full backup. Without the latter, the former is unusable.

- **Transaction log backup** – A copy of all log records inserted into the transaction log since the last log backup (or database checkpoint, if working in SIMPLE recovery model). When a log backup is made, the log generally gets truncated so that space in the file can be reused, although some factors can delay this (see Chapter 7). No inextricable link exists between a log backup and any specific full or differential database backup (unless it is the first full database backup). We can restore any full backup, followed by a complete chain of log backups, up to the required recovery point.

Some junior DBAs and many developers, perhaps misled by the term "full," assume that a full database backup backs up everything, both the data and contents of the transaction log. This is not correct. Essentially, both full and differential backups only back up the data files, although they do also back up enough of the transaction log to enable recovery of the backed up data, and reproduce any changes made while the backup was in progress. However, in practical terms, a full database backup **does not** back up the transaction log. We must take separate log backups for database restore purposes.

File and filegroup backups

For large databases, organized into multiple filegroups, it's possible to perform full and differential backups on individual filegroups, or files within those filegroups, rather than on the whole database. We won't discuss this topic further in this book, and will focus largely on log backups. For a fuller coverage of the topic of backups in general, including file backups, we can recommend Shawn McGehee's book (and free eBook), SQL Server Backup and Restore (HTTP://WWW.SIMPLE-TALK.COM/BOOKS/SQL-BOOKS/ SQL-BACKUP-AND-RESTORE/).

What Backups Do I Need to Take?

The overriding criterion for choosing which backups you need to take, and therefore which **recovery model** is required for a database (discussed shortly) is: *how much data loss is acceptable?*

Let's say that you rely exclusively on full backups, performing one every morning at 2 a.m., and the server experiences a fatal crash at 1 a.m. one morning. In this case, you would be able to restore the full database backup taken at 2 a.m. the previous morning, and you would have lost 23 hours-worth of data.

Let's now assume that you supplement the full database backup with a differential database backup, taken at 6 p.m., after work hours. In response to the crash, you'd restore the full backup followed by the differential and you will have lost 7 hours-worth of data.

All backups are I/O intensive processes, but this is especially true for full, and to a lesser extent differential, backups. They are likely to affect the performance of the database, and so we should avoid running them during times when users are accessing the database. In practical terms, if you rely only on full and differential backups, then the exposure to the risk of data loss for that database is going to be of the order of several hours.

If a database holds business-critical data and you would prefer to measure the exposure to data loss in minutes rather than hours, then you will need to take transaction log backups.

Let's finally assume that we supplement the full and differential backups with transaction log backups, taken every 30 minutes. In other words, we take a full database backup, followed by a series of transaction log backups, followed by a differential database backup, followed by a series of transaction log backups, followed by another full backup, and so on. Figure 3.1 shows a simplified picture of this (with a reduced number of log backups).

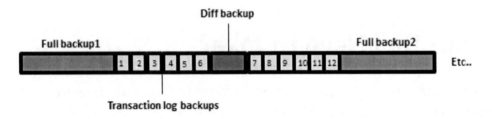

Figure 3.1:   A backup strategy comprising full and differential database backups and log backups.

In this case, we could restore the most recent full backup, the differential backup and the whole chain of log backups (files 7 to 12 in Figure 3.1) up to 12.30 a.m., and we would lose only 30 minutes-worth of data. In fact, if we still had access to the transaction log, we might be able to perform a **tail log backup** (covered in detail in Chapter 4) and minimize our data loss to close to zero. SQL Server will roll forward all of the actions recorded in the log backups, up to the specified point and then we can recover the database to a consistent state at a point in time very close to the time of the disaster.

Of course, this scheme assumes that all backups are valid and non-corrupt and, in the case of the log backups, that you have a full and complete **log chain**. We'll get to this in more detail shortly, but let's say that between the eighth and ninth log backups someone switched the database to SIMPLE recovery model, and then back to FULL, without taking any further backups. Upon switching to SIMPLE recovery model, SQL Server would have truncated the transaction log and we'd only be able to restore to the end of Log 8. In addition, any subsequent log backups would fail, until we took another full (or differential) database backup.

However, assuming this is not the case, then the scheme in Figure 3.1 offers much more "redundancy" to our restore options. If, for some reason, the differential backup is unavailable, we can restore the full backup followed by Logs 1–12. If Full Backup 1 was missing, we could even go back to the full backup before that, followed by the differential associated with that backup, followed by the long chain of log files, up to the required point.

Of course, with all these backups comes a much higher maintenance overhead, in terms of the extra effort of creating and monitoring the jobs required to run frequent transaction log backups, the I/O resources that these backups require (albeit for short periods of time), and the disk space required to store a large number of backup files. Due consideration needs to be given to this at a business level, before choosing the appropriate recovery model for a given database.

Database Recovery Models

SQL Server database backup and restore operations occur within the context of the **recovery model** of that database. A recovery model is a database property that determines whether you need, or are even able, to back up the log, and how SQL Server logs certain operations. This, in return, has implications for point-in-time restore operations. There are also some differences in the available restore operations, with regard to granular page and file restores, but we will not delve into that topic in this book.

In general, a database will be operating in either `SIMPLE` or `FULL` recovery model and the most important distinctions between the two are as follows:

- **SIMPLE** – SQL Server maintains the active log as normal, to support the needs of crash recovery and for rollback operations, as well as processes such as replication, database mirroring, and so on. However, log backup operations have no meaning since SQL Server truncates the log after each periodic checkpoint. Consequently, we cannot use the contents of the log to restore the database to a state in which it existed at some arbitrary previous point.

- **FULL** – SQL Server maintains the active log as normal and does not truncate the log after a database checkpoint. Only a log backup operation can truncate the log. SQL Server can apply log backups during database restore operations, essentially replaying (redoing) the operations therein, so that it can recover the database to the state in which it existed at a previous point in time.

There is also a third recovery model, BULK_LOGGED, in which certain operations that would normally generate a lot of writing to the log perform less logging, in order not to overwhelm the transaction log.

Choosing the right recovery model

In SIMPLE recovery model, only full and differential backups are possible. If this is sufficient to meet database recovery needs for that database, for example if this is a test database or it's largely read-only, then this is the model to use. However, if a database must support log restores, in order to meet the maximum permissible data loss requirements, or it needs log backups for some other reason (such as for log shipping), then we should operate that database in FULL recovery model, and implement regular log backups.

Don't forget that a full database backup does not result in truncation of the transaction log. For FULL and BULK_LOGGED recovery model databases, only a transaction log backup results in truncation of the log, so performing log backups is the only correct way to control the size of the log files in production systems (we'll discuss some of the common, but incorrect, ways in Chapter 7).

Temporarily, we may switch a database running in FULL recovery model to BULK_LOGGED model in order to run such operations with minimal logging, and then switch back to FULL model once those operations are complete. BULK_LOGGED recovery model is similar to FULL in that we can still run log backups, but if minimally logged operations are present in the log backup then this has implications for our ability to recover a database to a specific point in time. We will discuss this in a lot more detail in Chapter 6, but suffice to say for now that operating a database permanently in BULK_LOGGED model is not a viable way to minimize the size of transaction log.

Minimally logged operations

Examples of operations that SQL Server can minimally log include bulk import operations (using, for example, bcp or BULK INSERT)*,* SELECT/INTO *operations and certain index operations, such as index rebuilds. For a full list, see:* HTTP://MSDN.MICROSOFT.COM/EN-US/LIBRARY/MS191244.ASPX.

Setting the recovery model

The recovery model can be set using one of the simple commands shown in Listing 3.1.

```
USE master;

-- set recovery model to FULL
ALTER DATABASE TestDB
SET RECOVERY FULL;

-- set recovery model to SIMPLE
ALTER DATABASE TestDB
SET RECOVERY SIMPLE;

-- set recovery model to BULK_LOGGED
ALTER DATABASE TestDB
SET RECOVERY BULK_LOGGED;
```

Listing 3.1:   Setting the database recovery model.

A database will adopt the default recovery model specified by the model database. In many cases, this will mean that the default recovery model for a database is FULL, but different editions of SQL Server may have different defaults for the model database.

Discovering the recovery model

In theory, we can find out which model a given database is using by executing the query shown in Listing 3.2.

```
SELECT    name ,
          recovery_model_desc
FROM      sys.databases
WHERE     name = 'TestDB' ;
GO
```

Listing 3.2: Querying sys.databases for the recovery model.

However, be careful with this query, as it may not always tell the whole truth. For example, if we create a brand new database and then immediately run the command from Listing 3.2, it would report that the database was in FULL recovery model. However, in fact, **until we take a full database backup** the database will be operating in auto-truncate mode, sometimes referred to as pseudo-SIMPLE recovery model.

We can see this in action by creating a new database on a SQL Server 2008 instance, where the default recovery model is FULL. To make doubly sure, we explicitly set the recovery model to FULL and then query sys.databases to confirm, as shown in Listing 3.3.

```
/* STEP 1: CREATE THE DATABASE*/
USE master;
IF EXISTS ( SELECT   name
              FROM      sys.databases
              WHERE    name = 'TestDB' )
    DROP DATABASE TestDB;

CREATE DATABASE TestDB ON
(
  NAME = TestDB_dat,
  FILENAME = 'D:\SQLData\TestDB.mdf'
) LOG ON
(
  NAME = TestDB_log,
  FILENAME = 'D:\SQLData\TestDB.ldf'
);

/*STEP 2: Set the recovery model*/
ALTER DATABASE TestDB SET RECOVERY FULL;

/*STEP 3: Confirm the recovery model?*/
SELECT   name ,
         recovery_model_desc
FROM     sys.databases
WHERE    name = 'TestDB';
GO

/*OUTPUT:
name            recovery_model_desc
---------------------------------
TestDB          FULL
*/
```

Listing 3.3:   A newly created TestDB database, assigned the FULL recovery model.

This indicates that we're in FULL recovery model, so let's insert some data, check the log
space usage, force a checkpoint operation and then recheck the log usage, as shown in
Listing 3.4.

```
USE  TestDB
GO
IF  OBJECT_ID('dbo.PrimaryTable_Large ',  'U')  IS  NOT  NULL
     DROP  TABLE  dbo.PrimaryTable_Large;
SELECT  TOP  100000
         SomeColumn  =  'abcd ' ,
         Filler  =  REPLICATE('a',  200)
INTO     PrimaryTable_Large
FROM     msdb.sys.columns  a
         CROSS  JOIN  msdb.sys.columns  b
GO


DBCC  SQLPERF(LOGSPACE);


-- DBCC  SQLPERF  reports  a  24  MB  log  file  about  99%  full


CHECKPOINT
GO


DBCC  SQLPERF(LOGSPACE);
-- DBCC  SQLPERF  reports  a  24  MB  log  file  about  11%  full
```

Listing 3.4:   The log file is truncated on CHECKPOINT!

Note that the log file is roughly the same size after the checkpoint, but is only 11% full; because of the checkpoint operation, SQL Server truncated the log and made the space available for reuse.

Although the database is assigned to FULL recovery model, it is not actually operating in that model until the first full database backup is taken. Interestingly, this means we could have achieved the same effect by running that full backup of the TestDB database, instead of explicitly forcing a CHECKPOINT. The first full backup operation triggers a CHECKPOINT and the log is truncated. All full backups start by running a checkpoint. This is to ensure that as much of the changed data as possible is on disk, and to minimize the portion of the log that SQL Server needs to read at the end of the backup.

To tell for sure what recovery model is in operation, execute the query shown in
Listing 3.5.

```
SELECT     db_name(database_id) AS 'DatabaseName' ,
           last_log_backup_lsn
FROM       master.sys.database_recovery_status
WHERE      database_id = db_id('TestDB') ;
GO


DatabaseName                    last_log_backup_lsn
-------------------------------------------------
TestDB                NULL
```

Listing 3.5:   Is the database *really* in FULL recovery model?

If a value of NULL appears in the   column, then the database is actually in auto-
truncate mode, and so SQL Server will truncate the log when database checkpoints occur.
Having performed a full database backup, you will find that the column is populated
with the LSN of the log record that recorded the backup operation, and at this point the
database is truly in FULL recovery model. From this point on, a full database backup will
have **no effect** on the transaction log; the only way to truncate the log will be to back up
the log.

Switching models

If you ever switch a database from FULL or BULK LOGGED model to SIMPLE model, this
will break the log chain and you'll only be able to recover the database up to the point
of the last log backup taken before you switched. Therefore, always take that log backup
immediately before switching. If you subsequently switch the database back from SIMPLE
to FULL or BULK_LOGGED model, remember that the database will actually continue
operating in auto-truncate mode (Listing 3.5 will display NULL) until you perform another
full or differential backup.

If you switch from FULL to BULK_LOGGED model then this will *not* break the log chain. However, any bulk operations that occurred while in BULK_LOGGED model will not be fully logged in the transaction log and so cannot be controlled on an operation-by-operation basis, in the same way that fully logged operations can. This means that recovering a database to a point in time within a transaction log that contains bulk operations is *not* possible. You can only recover to the end of that log file. In order to "re-enable" point-in-time restore, switch back to FULL model after the bulk operation is complete and immediately take a log backup.

Log Backup Logistics

By now, I'm sure it's clear that, unless a database is operating in SIMPLE recovery model, it's vital that we take log backups. Furthermore, we must ensure that:

- we take log backups at a frequency that meets SLA requirements for permissible risk of data loss, and controls log growth

- we take steps to preserve the log chain, for use during restore operations

- all backups are stored securely

- we implement automated jobs to capture all required backups and verify those backups.

Frequency of log backups

The question of how frequently to back up the log file will depend on recovery requirements and the workload on the server. In critical financial or accounting applications, where the tolerance to data loss is more or less zero, it may be necessary to take log backups every 15 minutes, or perhaps even more frequently. In such cases, in order to avoid the need to restore a huge number of transaction log files, you may choose to adopt a backup scheme consisting of full backups interspersed with differential backups, interspersed with transaction log backups.

In reality, the backup scheme is often more of a compromise between the ideal and the practical, between an assessment of the true risk of data loss, and what it will cost the company, and the cost involved in mitigating that risk. Many very important business applications use somewhat simpler, but rigorous, backup schemes, perhaps involving regular nightly full backups coupled with hourly transaction log backups.

The transaction rate will also, to some extent, influence the frequency of log backups. For very busy databases, it may be necessary to back up more frequently in order to control the size of the log.

There is no easy way to calculate how often to take log backups. Most DBAs will take their best estimate at how often to take log backups, observe the growth characteristics of the files and then adjust the backup scheme as necessary to prevent them from getting oversized.

Preserving the log chain

As noted earlier, it is not possible to perform a transaction log backup without first taking at least one full backup. In order to recover a database to a point in time, either to the end of a particular log backup or to a point in time within a particular log backup, there must exist a full unbroken chain of log records, from the first log backup taken after a full (or differential backup), right up to the point of failure. This is the **log chain**.

There are many ways to break the log chain, and if you do, it means that you will only be able to recover the database to the time of the log backup taken before the event occurred that broke the chain. In short, breaking the chain is **not** a good idea if you care about the ability to restore your data. Below are two of the most common ways to break the chain.

- **Loss or corruption of a transaction log backup file** – You will only be able to recover to the last preceding good log backup. The log chain will start again at the next good full or differential backup.

- **Switch to SIMPLE recovery model** – If you ever switch from FULL to SIMPLE recovery model, this will break the log chain, as SQL Server instigates a checkpoint and truncates the transaction log immediately. When and if you return to FULL model, you will need to take another full backup to restart the log chain, or a differential backup to bridge the LSN gap that will now exist. In fact, until you take that full or differential backup, the database will remain in auto-truncate mode and you won't be able to back up the log file.

Pre-SQL Server 2008, there were a couple of commands, namely BACKUP LOG WITH NO_LOG or BACKUP LOG WITH TRUNCATE_ONLY (they are functionally equivalent) that would force a log file truncation and so break the log chain. You should not issue these commands in any version of SQL Server, but we mention them here as many still use them, when trying to deal with a "runaway log file," without understanding their implications for database restore. See Chapter 7 for more details.

Storing log backups

Clearly, the data and log backup files should not be stored on the same drive that hosts the data or log files. If either of those drives suffers hardware failure then the backups will be lost too. The backup files should be stored on a separate device, or backed up to a local, mirrored drive. A common scheme might involve initial backup to local disk storage, followed by copying the files to a redundant network storage (and finally to an offsite tape backup library).

Automating and verifying backups

We can perform ad hoc database and transaction log backups via simple T-SQL scripts in SQL Server Management Studio. However, for production systems, the DBA will need a way to automate these backups, and verify that the backups are valid, via a combination of validation checks and test restores.

In-depth coverage of this topic is outside the scope of this book, and we refer you to Shawn McGehee' s book, *SQL Server Backup and Restore* (HTTP://WWW.SIMPLE-TALK.COM/ BOOKS/SQL-BOOKS/SQL-BACKUP-AND-RESTORE/), for fuller treatment.

Here, we simply list some of the available options. Due to some of the shortcomings of the SSMS Maintenance Plans, most experienced DBAs would opt to write their own scripts and then automate them.

- **SSMS Maintenance Plans Wizard and Designer** – Two tools, built into SSMS, which allow us to configure and schedule a range of database maintenance tasks, including full database backups and transaction log backups. The DBA can also run DBCC integrity checks, schedule jobs to remove old backup files, and so on. An excellent description of these tools and their limitations can be found in Brad McGehee's book, *Brad's Sure Guide to SQL Server Maintenance Plans* (HTTP://WWW.AMAZON.COM/ BRADS-GUIDE-SERVER-MAINTENANCE-HANDBOOKS/DP/1906434344).

- **T-SQL scripts** – We can write custom T-SQL scripts to automate our backup tasks. Ola Hallengren (HTTP://OLA.HALLENGREN.COM/) provides and maintains a well-established and respected set of maintenance scripts. These scripts, which create a variety of stored procedures, each performing a specific database maintenance task including backups, are automated using SQL Agent jobs.

- **PowerShell/SMO scripting** – More powerful and versatile than T-SQL scripting, but with a steeper learning curve for many DBAs, PowerShell can be used to script and automate almost any maintenance task.
  See, for example: HTTP://WWW.SIMPLE-TALK.COM/AUTHOR/ALLEN-WHITE/ or
  HTTP://WWW.SIMPLE-TALK.COM/AUTHOR/LAERTE-JUNIOR/.

- **Third-party backup tools** – Several third-party tools exist that can automate backups, as well as verify and monitor them. Most offer backup compression and encryption as well as additional features to ease backup management, verify backups, and so on. See, for example, Red Gate's SQL Backup:
  (HTTP://WWW.RED-GATE.COM/PRODUCTS/DBA/SQL-BACKUP/).

Summary

In this chapter, we discussed the importance of devising the right backup regime for the needs of your most important production databases. Most of these databases will be operating in FULL recovery model, with regular log backups alongside full and, possibly, differential database backups. These backups are vital, not only for database restore and recovery, but also for controlling the size of the transaction log.

Some databases don't require point-in-time restore, or need the log backups for any other purpose (such as database mirroring), and have data-loss objectives which can be met with full and differential database backups only. In these cases, we can operate them in SIMPLE recovery model, greatly simplifying log maintenance.

We also briefly discussed log backup logistics, and the need to automate log backups, schedule them at the right frequency, verify them, and store them securely.

In Chapter 4, we begin a series of three chapters examining in more detail log management in each of the three database recovery levels, starting with SIMPLE.

Chapter 4: Managing the Log in SIMPLE Recovery Model

This chapter title is almost a misnomer because, to a large degree, working in SIMPLE model negates the need to manage the transaction log. As such, this will be the shortest chapter in the book!

In SIMPLE recovery model, the sole purpose of the transaction log is to guarantee data consistency and integrity during normal day-to-day operation, providing a means to return the database to a consistent state in the event of error or transaction rollback, or during crash recovery. We cannot back up the transaction log for databases working in SIMPLE recovery model, so log backups play no part in any restore operations.

Working in SIMPLE Recovery Model

In SIMPLE recovery model, SQL Server still logs all transactions, but will minimally log certain bulk operations; in effect, the level of logging is the same as that applied in BULK_LOGGED model (Chapter 6).

Any log record relating to an open transaction, or one that is required to remain in the log by another database process, in other words, any log record that is higher (more recent) than MinLSN (see Chapter 2) will remain in the active log. Whenever a database in SIMPLE model restarts, the recovery process will kick in and the data files will be reconciled with the contents of the transaction log, any changes resulting from incomplete transactions will be rolled back, and so on.

However, in SIMPLE model, SQL Server truncates (marks as inactive) any VLFs that contain no part of the active log, during regular database checkpoints. As a result, SQL Server reuses space in the transaction log regularly and routinely.

A database in **SIMPLE** recovery model is always in **auto-truncate** mode. As noted in Chapter 3, all user databases, even those designated as operating in **FULL** recovery model, will be in auto-truncate mode until we perform the first full database backup.

How often do checkpoints happen?

*The SQL Server engine decides how often to perform a checkpoint based on how many log records it will need to process in order to recover a database in the time specified by the **recovery interval** server configuration option. If your database is mainly read-only, the time between checkpoints may be long. However, on busy, frequently updated systems, checkpoints can occur about every minute. See* HTTP://MSDN.MICROSOFT.COM/EN-GB/LIBRARY/MS189573.ASPX *for more details.*

While SQL Server still writes to the log a complete description of all actions performed, it does not retain them such that log backups can capture this complete description. The LSN chain will be incomplete. In short, log backups have no meaning in **SIMPLE** recovery model and, in fact, we cannot even perform transaction log backups, as Listing 4.1 demonstrates.

```
USE master;
ALTER DATABASE TestDB
SET RECOVERY SIMPLE;

BACKUP Log TestDB
TO DISK ='D:\SQLBackups\TestDB_log.trn'
GO

Msg 4208, Level 16, State 1, Line 1
The statement BACKUP LOG is not allowed while the recovery model is SIMPLE. Use BACKUP
DATABASE or change the recovery model using ALTER DATABASE.
Msg 3013, Level 16, State 1, Line 1
BACKUP LOG is terminating abnormally.
```

Listing 4.1:   You can't perform log backups in **SIMPLE** model.

This means that our backup and restore scheme will consist entirely of full (and possibly differential) database backups.

Pros and Cons of SIMPLE Recovery Model

The downside to working in SIMPLE model, of course, is that the exposure to the risk of data loss might be quite high, as we can only restore a database to the time of the most recent full or differential backup. As noted previously, if you wish to measure exposure to data loss in minutes rather than hours, don't use SIMPLE model.

However, if you are running a development or test database, or perhaps even a production database that is mainly read-only, then using SIMPLE model may well be a viable and even sensible option, and will greatly ease the maintenance burdens on that database. Less backup storage space will be required, and subsequent restore operations will be much simpler. Furthermore, since the transaction log is auto-truncated, there is less exposure to the risk of it growing out of control, and potentially causing 9002 errors.

Although, SIMPLE model significantly eases the burden of transaction log management, it's a mistake to assume that, if you're using this model, you can completely forget about managing the log. The transaction log is still playing a vital role in the day-to-day operation of the database, and you still need to size and grow the transaction log appropriately, according to the nature and frequency of transactions on that database. Just because the log is auto-truncated, it does not mean that hefty and long-running transactions cannot cause the log to expand rapidly, and cause you trouble if you haven't sized it correctly – more on this in Chapter 7.

Chapter 5: Managing the Log in FULL Recovery Model

We'll start by taking a deeper look at log backups, including tail log backups, for databases in FULL recovery model and then at how to perform various database restore operations using these log backup files, in conjunction with full database backups.

FULL recovery model supports database restore to any point in time within an available log backup and, assuming we have a tail log backup, right up to the time of the last committed transaction before the failure occurred.

What Gets Logged?

In FULL recovery model, SQL Server fully logs all operations, meaning that it logs a set of records containing enough information, either at the page or row level, to make a roll forward possible. Certain of these log records will record the ID of the transaction that performed the statement, and when that transaction started and ended.

Operations that SQL Server can minimally log, such as SELECT INTO, BULK INSERT and CREATE INDEX, are still fully logged when working in FULL recovery model, but SQL Server does it slightly differently. It does not log individually the rows affected by those operations. Instead, it logs only the data pages, as they get filled. This reduces the logging overhead of such operations, while making sure that there still exists all the information required to perform rollback, redo and point-in-time restores.

Kalen Delaney has published some investigations into logging for SELECT INTO (HTTP://SQLBLOG.COM/BLOGS/KALEN_DELANEY/ARCHIVE/2011/03/15/WHAT-GETS-LOGGED-FOR-SELECT-INTO.ASPX) and index rebuild (HTTP://SQLBLOG.COM/BLOGS/KALEN_DELANEY/ARCHIVE/2011/03/08/WHAT-GETS-LOGGED-FOR-INDEX-REBUILDS.ASPX) operations, both in FULL and BULK_LOGGED recovery models. The differences in logging of minimally logged operations, when working in BULK_LOGGED model, are discussed in more detail in Chapter 6.

Basics of Log Backup

First things first: are all of our FULL recovery model databases receiving log backups? Probably the most common cause of transaction log-related issues is working in FULL recovery model and not taking log backups, or taking log backups too infrequently to control the size of the transaction log file.

If this is the case, then we need to investigate whether these databases really need to use FULL recovery, and if so, we need to start taking log backups. In this section, we'll cover basic log backup commands, including how to take tail log backups.

Are log backups being taken?

If we are unsure whether there are any transaction log backups for a given database, then we can simply interrogate the backupset table in the MSDB database (HTTP://MSDN.MICROSOFT.COM/EN-US/LIBRARY/MS186299.ASPX), using a query similar to that shown in Listing 5.1.

```
USE msdb ;
SELECT    backup_set_id ,
          backup_start_date ,
          backup_finish_date ,
          backup_size ,
          recovery_model ,
          [type]
FROM      dbo.backupset
WHERE     database_name = 'TestDB'
```

Listing 5.1:   Are log backups being taken?

In the `type` column, a `D` represents a database backup, `L` represents a log backup, and `I` represents a differential backup.

Note that, since the data in this `backupset` table could be manipulated without affecting backup and restore behavior, it's wise to verify findings from this query. We can do this either by querying `sys.database_recovery_status` to see the value of `last_log_backup_lsn` (see Listing 3.5), or the `sys.databases` table to see the value of `log_reuse_wait_desc` (will return `LOG_BACKUP` if a backup is required).

How to back up the transaction log

As discussed previously, it is not possible to perform a transaction log backup without first taking at least one full backup. In fact, if we have a database that is in **FULL** recovery model, but which we've never backed up, then it will not actually be working in **FULL** recovery model. The database will be in auto-truncate mode until we run the first full backup.

We perform all database backups, full, log, or otherwise, using the **BACKUP** command. The command accepts numerous options, which are documented here: HTTP://MSDN. MICROSOFT.COM/EN-US/LIBRARY/MS186865.ASPX. However, at its most basic, the command to perform a full backup to disk is as follows:

```
BACKUP DATABASE DatabaseName
TO DISK ='FileLocation\DatabaseName.bak';
```

If this were the first database backup of this name, SQL Server would create the `DatabaseName.bak` file in the specified directory. If such a file already existed, then the default behavior is to append subsequent backups to that file. To override this behavior, and stipulate that SQL Server should overwrite any existing file, we can use the `INIT` option, as follows:

```
BACKUP DATABASE DatabaseName
TO DISK ='FileLocation\DatabaseName.bak'
WITH INIT;
```

Of course, during a normal backup regime, we do not want to overwrite existing backups. When used in this book, it is simply a convenience to facilitate repeatable tests.

Most commonly, we'd give each subsequent backup a unique name; more on this in the forthcoming section, *Full restore to point of failure*.

After each regular (e.g. daily) full backup, there will be frequent (e.g. hourly) log backups, the basic command for which is very similar:

```
BACKUP LOG DatabaseName
TO DISK ='FileLocation\DatabaseName_Log.trn';
```

Tail log backups

As long as we have a recent full backup and a complete log chain, we can recover our database to the state in which it existed at the end of the final log backup before any failure. However, suppose that we take transaction log backups hourly, on the hour, and a failure occurs at 1:45 p.m. We could potentially lose 45 minutes-worth of data.

Let's say that at 1:45 p.m. a drive hosting the secondary data file failed; the database is still online and we still have access to the transaction log, contained on a separate, dedicated array. In such a situation, we can perform a special form of log backup, a **tail log backup**, which will capture the remaining contents of the transaction log, and place the damaged database in a restoring state, as follows:

```
BACKUP LOG DatabaseName
TO DISK ='FileLocation\DatabaseName_Log_tail.trn'
WITH NORECOVERY
```

The `NORECOVERY` option puts the database in a restoring state, ensures that no further transactions will succeed after the tail log backup, and assumes that the next action we wish to perform is a `RESTORE`. We can then restore our full database (or file) backups, followed by the full chain of log backups, finishing with the tail log backup, and then recover the database.

However, let's say instead that the 1:45 p.m. failure causes damage so bad that the database will not come back online. In this case, a normal log backup (or a tail log backup using `WITH NORECOVERY`) will fail because it will attempt to truncate the log and, as part of that operation, it needs to write into the database's header the new log `MinLSN`.

In such cases, we can still attempt to back up the tail of the log, using the `NO_TRUNCATE` option instead of the `NORECOVERY` option.

```
BACKUP LOG DatabaseName
TO DISK ='FileLocation\DatabaseName_Log_tail.trn'
WITH NO_TRUNCATE
```

Note that we should only use this option if a failure has damaged the database severely and it won't come online.

Tail log backups and minimally logged operations

If the data files are unavailable because of the database failure, and the tail of the log contains minimally logged operations, then it will not be possible to do a tail log backup, as this would require access to the changed data extents in the data file. This will be covered in more detail in Chapter 6, Managing the Log in BULK_LOGGED Recovery Model.

Performing Restore and Recovery

Having performed a tail log backup, the next step is to restore the last full backup (followed by differential backup, if appropriate), then restore the complete sequence of log backup files, including the tail log backup. The basic syntax for this sequence of restore operations is as follows:

```
RESTORE {DATABASE | LOG} DatabaseName
FROM DISK ='FileLocation\FileName.bak'
WITH NORECOVERY;
```

After each restore operation we perform using the WITH NORECOVERY option, SQL Server will roll forward the contents of the applied log backups, and leave the database in a restoring state, ready to accept further log backups.

If we omit the WITH NORECOVERY option, then by default the RESTORE command will proceed WITH RECOVERY. In other words, SQL Server will reconcile the data and log files, rolling forward completed transactions and then rolling back uncompleted transactions as necessary. After restoring the last backup in the restore sequence, we can then restore WITH RECOVERY and SQL Server will perform the necessary roll forward and roll back to recover the database to a consistent state.

```
RESTORE DATABASE DatabaseName
WITH RECOVERY
```

A common requirement is to restore the database to a different location, in which case you can simply move the files as part of the restore process, as described here: HTTP://MSDN.MICROSOFT.COM/EN-US/LIBRARY/MS190255.ASPX, and demonstrated later in the chapter.

Full restore to point of failure

Assuming that we can still reach the transaction log after a database failure, caused perhaps by a hardware failure, then in theory it should be possible to restore and recover our database right up to the point of failure, by using the following steps:

1. Back up the tail of the log.

2. Restore the most recent full backup (plus differential, if applicable).

3. Restore, in turn, each of the transaction log backups that were taken after the full (or differential) backup and completed before the time of failure.

4. Restore the tail log backup.

5. Recover the database.

Many of the examples found on Books Online demonstrate restore and recovery from a "backup set," in other words a single "device" where all backups are stored. In practical terms, this means that, when backing up to disk, the backup device is a single .bak file located somewhere on that disk.

For example, the simple example shown in Listing 5.2 uses a backup set consisting of one full backup and one transaction log backup, and shows how to perform a full restore. In order to run this code, you'll first need to re-create the TestDB database and then insert a few sample rows of data (for convenience, the script to do this, **CreateAndPopulateTestDB.sql**, is included with the code download for this chapter). As usual, you'll also need to have a **SQLBackups** directory on the local **D:** drive of your database server, or modify the file paths as appropriate. This example assumes that the database is still online when we perform the tail log backup.

```
-- Perform a full backup of the Test database
-- The WITH FORMAT option starts a new backup set
-- Be careful, as it will overwrite any existing sets
-- The full backup becomes the first file in the set
BACKUP DATABASE TestDB
TO DISK = 'D:\SQLBackups\TestDB.bak'
WITH FORMAT;
GO


-- Perform a transaction log backup of the Test database
-- This is the second file in the set
BACKUP Log TestDB
TO DISK = 'D:\SQLBackups\TestDB.bak'
GO


-- ....<FAILURE OCCURS HERE>....


-- The RESTORE HEADERONLY command is optional.
-- It simply confirms the files that comprise
-- the current set
RESTORE HEADERONLY
FROM DISK = 'D:\SQLBackups\TestDB.bak'
GO


-- Back up the tail of the log to prepare for restore
-- This will become the third file of the backup set
BACKUP Log TestDB
TO DISK = 'D:\SQLBackups\TestDB.bak'
WITH NORECOVERY;
GO
```

```
-- Restore the full backup
RESTORE DATABASE TestDB
FROM DISK = 'D:\SQLBackups\TestDB.bak'
WITH FILE=1, NORECOVERY;

-- Apply the transaction log backup
RESTORE LOG TestDB
FROM DISK = 'D:\SQLBackups\TestDB.bak'
WITH FILE=2, NORECOVERY;-- Apply the tail log backup
RESTORE LOG TestDB
FROM DISK = 'D:\SQLBackups\TestDB.bak'
WITH FILE=3, NORECOVERY;

-- Recover the database
RESTORE DATABASE TestDB
WITH RECOVERY;
GO
```

Listing 5.2:   Backing up to, and restoring from, a backup set; not recommended.

However, using backup sets seems to be a relic from times when we backed up databases to tape. When backing up to disk, it is a bad idea to use this scheme because, of course, the backup file will quickly grow very large.

In practice, it is far more common that each full backup and transaction log backup file will be individually named, and probably stamped with the time and date we took the backup. For example, most third-party backup tools, popular community-generated scripts, plus the maintenance plan wizard /designer in SSMS, will all create separate date-stamped files e.g. **AdventureWorks_FULL_20080904_000001.bak**. For all further examples, we'll adopt the scheme of uniquely named backups.

Restore to end of log backup

Sometimes, we only wish to restore to the end of a certain log backup or, if the transaction log is unavailable because of a failure, then we may have no choice!

To set up this example, run Listing 5.2, which creates a **FullRecovery** database, operating in **FULL** recovery model, and performs a full database backup.

```
USE master
GO
IF DB_ID('FullRecovery') IS NOT NULL
    DROP DATABASE FullRecovery;
GO

-- Clear backup history
EXEC msdb.dbo.sp_delete_database_backuphistory @database_name = N'FullRecovery'
GO

CREATE DATABASE FullRecovery ON
(NAME = FullRecovery_dat,
  FILENAME = 'D:\SQLData\FullRecovery.mdf'
) LOG ON
(
  NAME = FullRecovery_log,
  FILENAME = 'D:\SQLData\FullRecovery.ldf'
);

ALTER DATABASE FullRecovery SET RECOVERY FULL
GO

BACKUP DATABASE FullRecovery TO DISK = 'D:\SQLBackups\FullRecovery.bak'
WITH INIT
GO
```

Listing 5.3:   Create the **FullRecovery** database, operating in **FULL** recovery model.

In Listing 5.4, we create the **SomeTable** table, insert some data, and then take a log backup.

```
USE FullRecovery
GO
IF OBJECT_ID('dbo.SomeTable', 'U') IS NOT NULL
    DROP TABLE dbo.SomeTable
GO
CREATE TABLE SomeTable
    (
       SomeInt INT IDENTITY ,
       SomeCol VARCHAR(5)
    );

INSERT  INTO SomeTable
        ( SomeCol
        )
        SELECT TOP ( 10 )
                REPLICATE('a', 5)
        FROM    sys.columns AS c;

BACKUP LOG FullRecovery TO DISK = 'D:\SQLBackups\FullRecovery_log.trn'
WITH INIT
GO
```

Listing 5.4:   Create and populate **SomeTable**, in the **FullRecovery** database, and run a log backup.

Finally, in Listing 5.5, we update a row in **SomeTable**, make a note of the time immediately afterwards (we'll need this for a later restore), and then perform a named, marked transaction (again, more on this shortly) which accidentally empties **SomeTable**.

```
/*UPDATE a row in the SomeTable*/
UPDATE   dbo.SomeTable
SET      SomeCol = 'bbbbb'
WHERE    SomeInt = 1

SELECT GETDATE();
/*Note this date down, as we'll need it later
2012-10-05 16:23:06.740*/

/*A named, marked transaction with a missing WHERE clause*/
BEGIN TRANSACTION Delete_SomeTable WITH MARK
DELETE dbo.SomeTable;
COMMIT TRANSACTION Delete_SomeTable
```

Listing 5.5:   Update a row in SomeTable then delete the table contents in a marked transaction.

For this example, we're simply going to restore over the top of the existing
FullRecovery database, to return it to the state in which it existed at the time
of the log backup. Listing 5.6 restores our full database backup over the top of the
existing database and then applies the log backup.

```
USE master
GO
--restore the full database backup
RESTORE DATABASE FullRecovery
FROM DISK='D:\SQLBackups\FullRecovery.bak'
WITH NORECOVERY;

--restore the log backup
RESTORE LOG FullRecovery
FROM DISK='D:\SQLBackups\FullRecovery_log.trn'
WITH RECOVERY;
```

Listing 5.6:   Restoring to the end of the log backup (no tail log backup).

In this case, however, we'll get a useful and descriptive error.

```
Msg 3159, Level 16, State 1, Line 1
The tail of the log for the database "FullRecovery" has not been backed up. Use BACKUP LOG
WITH NORECOVERY to back up the log if it contains work you do not want to lose. Use the WITH
REPLACE or WITH STOPAT clause of the RESTORE statement to just overwrite the contents of the
log.
Msg 3013, Level 16, State 1, Line 1
RESTORE DATABASE is terminating abnormally.
Msg 3117, Level 16, State 1, Line 5
The log or differential backup cannot be restored because no files are ready to rollforward.
Msg 3013, Level 16, State 1, Line 5
RESTORE DATABASE is terminating abnormally.
```

SQL Server is warning us that we're about to overwrite the transaction log of the existing
FullRecovery database, and we have not done a tail log backup, so any operations in
there would be lost forever. In this example, it means that after the proposed restore
operation we'd lose forever the effects of Listing 5.5, which we haven't backed up. If we're
certain that we don't need to perform that backup, we can override this check using
WITH REPLACE when we restore the full backup, as follows, and then perform the log
restore as normal.

```
RESTORE DATABASE FullRecovery
FROM DISK='D:\SQLBackups\FullRecovery.bak'
WITH NORECOVERY, REPLACE;
```

Conversely, only use REPLACE when certain that a tail log backup is not required. In this
example, we'll take that tail log backup, even though we don't need it right away. This
pitches the database into a restoring state and we proceed immediately with the restore
operation, as shown in Listing 5.7.

```
USE master
GO
BACKUP LOG FullRecovery
TO DISK='D:\SQLBackups\FullRecovery_tail.trn'
WITH INIT, NORECOVERY;

USE master
GO
RESTORE DATABASE FullRecovery
FROM DISK='D:\SQLBackups\FullRecovery.bak'
WITH NORECOVERY;

RESTORE DATABASE FullRecovery
FROM DISK='D:\SQLBackups\FullRecovery_log.trn'
WITH RECOVERY;

USE FullRecovery
SELECT TOP 1 * FROM SomeTable
```

	SomeInt	SomeCol
1	1	aaaaa

Listing 5.7:   A tail log backup followed by a restore operation.

As you can see, we've returned the database to the state in which it existed after the first log backup. Of course, we could restore the database to the end of the tail log backup, as shown in Listing 5.8, but then we'd just be returning the database to the state where all data had been lost from SomeTable.

```
-- This time we don't want to back up the tail, so use REPLACE
USE master
GO
RESTORE DATABASE FullRecovery
FROM DISK='D:\SQLBackups\FullRecovery.bak'
WITH NORECOVERY, REPLACE;

RESTORE LOG FullRecovery
FROM DISK='D:\SQLBackups\FullRecovery_log.trn'
WITH NORECOVERY;

RESTORE LOG FullRecovery
FROM DISK='D:\SQLBackups\FullRecovery_tail.trn'
WITH RECOVERY;
```

Listing 5.8: A full restore operation.

Query SomeTable and you'll see that there is no data. Let's now see how to get it back; in order to do this, we'll need to stop our restore operation after the update in Listing 5.5, but before the rogue delete.

Point-in-time restores

Whether DBAs like it or not, developers often have access to production databases to perform ad hoc data loads and changes. It is the joint responsibility of the DBA and the developer to ensure these proceed smoothly, but accidents can and do happen, and may result in the accidental deletion or modification of data. In such an event, the DBA may need to perform a point-in-time restore, to return a database to the state in which it existed prior to the rogue transaction, and then copy the lost data back into the production database. We'll cover two such techniques to perform a point-time restore:

- **RESTORE...WITH...STOPBEFOREMARK** – restoring to a marked transaction.

- **RESTORE...WITH...STANDBY** – restoring a standby database to specific point in time.

Of course, the exact nature of the reparative action required depends on the nature of the "bad" transaction. If someone accidentally dropped a table, and we don't know exactly when it happened, then it's possible we'll be heading down the RESTORE WITH STANDBY route. At other times, we may get away with simply creating a script to "reverse out" the rogue modifications. If the damage affected only a single column, or a limited number of rows, then it may be possible, as an alternative, to use a tool such as SQL Data Compare, which can compare directly to backup files, and can do row-level restores.

If we have SQL Server 2005 (or later) Enterprise Edition plus a recent database snapshot, we may be able to run a query against the snapshot to retrieve the data as it looked at the time the database snapshot was taken. We can then write an UPDATE or INSERT command to pull the data from the database snapshot into the live, source database.

Finally, as a last resort, a specialized log reader tool may help us reverse out the effects of a transaction, although I'm not aware of any that work reliably in SQL Server 2005 and later.

However, the ultimate safeguard, and most likely route to restoring the database without losing any data, is to have a complete set of backups, and to use them to perform a point-in-time restore.

Point-in-time restore to a marked transaction

A wise DBA can use marked transactions to create an easy recovery point, prior to deploying a large set of changes to a database, in cases where the potential for problems exists. Sadly, it is rare that a user, who mistakenly drops, truncates, or deletes a table will have been kind enough to use a marked transaction, but in this case, they have, and so we can use this fact to get our data back.

In this example, rather than restore over the top of a live database, we'll create a separate copy of the database, alongside the current FullRecovery database. Listing 5.9 restores our full backup to create the FullRecovery_Copy database.

```
USE master
GO
IF DB_ID('FullRecovery_Copy') IS NOT NULL
    DROP DATABASE FullRecovery_Copy;
GO
RESTORE DATABASE FullRecovery_Copy
FROM  DISK = N'D:\SQLBackups\FullRecovery.bak'
WITH
MOVE N'FullRecovery_Dat' TO N'D:\SQLDATA\FullRecovery_Copy.mdf',
MOVE N'FullRecovery_Log' TO N'D:\SQLDATA\FullRecovery_Copy.ldf',
NORECOVERY
GO
```

Listing 5.9:   Restore the full database backup for FullRecovery to create FullRecovery_Copy.

We've left the FullRecovery_Copy database in a restoring state, and the next step is to restore the first log backup, using **WITH...STOPBEFOREMARK**, because we want to return our database to a consistent state as of the last committed transaction at the time the marked transaction started.

```
RESTORE LOG [FullRecovery_Copy]
FROM  DISK = N'D:\SQLBackups\FullRecovery_Log.trn'
WITH
   NORECOVERY,
   STOPBEFOREMARK = N'Delete_SomeTable'
GO
```

Listing 5.10:   Restoring FullRecovery_Copy to a marked transaction, Step 1.

At this point, we'll see the following message since the log backup does not contain the designated mark:

```
Processed 0 pages for database 'FullRecovery_Copy', file 'FullRecovery_dat' on file 1.
Processed 4 pages for database 'FullRecovery_Copy', file 'FullRecovery_log' on file 1.
This log file contains records logged before the designated mark. The database is being left
in the Restoring state so you can apply another log file.
RESTORE LOG successfully processed 4 pages in 0.007 seconds (4.115 MB/sec).
```

In this example, the tail log backup contains our marked transaction and so, in Listing 5.11, we restore that tail log backup.

```
RESTORE LOG [FullRecovery_Copy]
FROM  DISK = N'D:\SQLBackups\FullRecovery_tail.trn'
WITH
      NORECOVERY,
      STOPBEFOREMARK = N'Delete_SomeTable'
GO
```

Listing 5.11:   Restoring `FullRecovery_Copy` to a marked transaction, Step 2.

This time the message is as follows:

```
Processed 0 pages for database 'FullRecovery_Copy', file 'FullRecovery_dat' on file 1.
Processed 5 pages for database 'FullRecovery_Copy', file 'FullRecovery_log' on file 1.
RESTORE LOG successfully processed 5 pages in 0.008 seconds (4.699 MB/sec)
```

At this point, we can recover the `FullRecovery_Copy` database and query it, as shown in Listing 5.12.

```
RESTORE DATABASE [FullRecovery_Copy]
WITH  RECOVERY
GO

USE FullRecovery_copy
SELECT TOP 1 * FROM SomeTable
```

	SomeInt	SomeCol
1	1	bbbbb

Listing 5.12:   Restoring `FullRecovery_Copy` to a marked transaction, final step.

As you can see, our restored copy of the database contains the effects of our update, but not the accidental delete. We can now think about copying the contents of `SomeTable` back into our production copy of the `FullRecovery` database (we'll discuss this in more detail in the next section).

Point-in-time restore to a standby database

For our final example, let's assume that this accidental delete was not a marked transaction and that we don't know exactly when this unfortunate event occurred. Our response to such a situation would depend on the nature of the problem. If possible, we might disconnect all users from the database (after notifying them), and assess the implications of what just happened. In some cases, we might need to estimate the time the problem occurred and then do a full recovery of the database and logs using a point-in-time restore. Having done the restore, we'd have to notify users that some transactions might have been lost, and ask for forgiveness.

Often, of course, we will not be able to interrupt normal business operation in this manner, to fix an accidental data loss. Since the live database is still running and users are accessing it, we could try restoring a backup of the database in **STANDBY** mode. This allows us to restore further log backups but, unlike when using **NORECOVERY**, the database is still readable.

The restore scheme might look something like this:

1. Restore a backup of the database, in **STANDBY** mode, alongside the live database.

2. Roll the logs forward to the point just before the bad transaction occurred, and data was lost.

3. Copy the lost data across to the live database and drop the restored copy.

Of course, this process is not necessarily straightforward, and can be quite time-consuming. Unless we've purchased a specialized log reading tool, and can interrogate the log backup directly, rolling the logs forward can mean a series of painstaking steps involving restoring a log, checking the data, restoring a bit further, and so on, until we've worked out exactly where the bad transaction occurred. Step 3 can be difficult, too, since we will be introducing data into the live system that is not necessarily consistent with the current state of the database, so there could be referential integrity issues.

Nevertheless, let's look at how this works. In order to try to retrieve the lost data without interrupting normal business operation, we're going to restore our backups to create a Standby_FullRecovery database, in STANDBY mode.

```
USE master
GO
IF DB_ID('Standby_FullRecovery') IS NOT NULL
    DROP DATABASE Standby_FullRecovery;
GO
RESTORE DATABASE Standby_FullRecovery
FROM  DISK = N'D:\SQLBackups\FullRecovery.bak'
WITH
  MOVE N'FullRecovery_Dat' TO N'D:\SQLDATA\Standby_FullRecovery.mdf',
  MOVE N'FullRecovery_Log' TO N'D:\SQLDATA\Standby_FullRecovery.ldf',
  STANDBY =
        N'D:\SQLBackups\Standby_FullRecovery_Copy_UNDO.bak'
GO
```

Listing 5.13:   Restoring the full backup for FullRecovery to create a standby database.

We now have a new database, called Standby_FullRecovery, and it's in "Standby / Read-Only" mode, as shown in Figure 5.1. As you can see, there are currently no user tables.

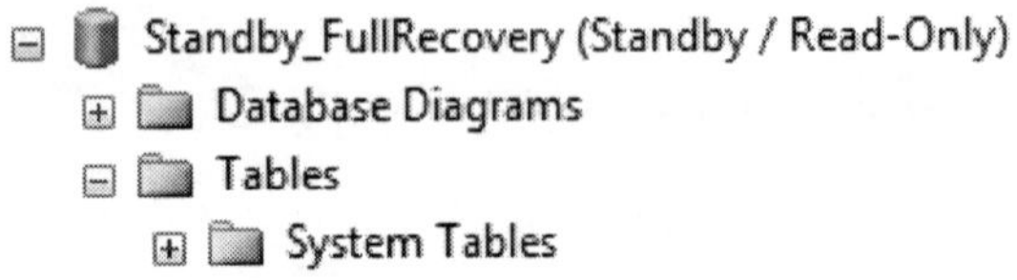

Figure 5.1:   The standby database.

The next step is to restore the first log backup to the standby-mode database. In doing so, we must create an undo file for the standby database. This undo file contains information relating to which operations in the log backup SQL Server had to undo during the restore operation, in order to make the database readable. When the next log backup is applied, SQL Server first has to "redo" whatever undo is stored in the undo file.

```
RESTORE LOG Standby_FullRecovery
FROM   DISK = N'D:\SQLBackups\Fullrecovery_Log.trn'
WITH
       STANDBY =
          N'D:\SQLBackups\Standby_FullRecovery_Copy_UNDO.bak'
    --    STOPAT = '2012-10-05 16:23:06.740'
GO
```

Listing 5.14: Restore the first log backup to the standby database.

Next, we can restore fully the next log backup (in this example, the tail log backup). Having done so, we'll find that all the data in `SomeTable` is gone, and so we know that this log backup contains the rogue delete transaction. Fortunately, in this case, not only do we know that already, we also know the exact time we wish to stop the restore. Therefore, we can proceed as shown in Listing 5.15, restoring the tail log backup using `WITH STOPAT` to stop the restore at the point of the last committed transaction, at the time specified, just before we lost the data.

```
USE master
Go
RESTORE LOG Standby_FullRecovery
FROM   DISK = N'D:\SQLBackups\Fullrecovery_tail.trn'
WITH
       STANDBY =
          N'D:\SQLBackups\Standby_FullRecovery_Copy_UNDO.bak',
       STOPAT = '2012-10-05 16:23:06.740'
GO
```

Listing 5.15: Restoring the tail log backup to a specified point in time.

Query the `Standby_FullRecovery` database and you'll see that the lost data is back, and we can attempt to reintroduce it to the live database, as discussed earlier.

Of course, the less sure we are of the exact time to which we need to restore, the trickier the process can become. Aside from third-party log readers (very few of which offer support beyond SQL Server 2005), there are a couple of undocumented and unsupported functions that can be used to interrogate the contents of log files (`fn_dblog`) and log backups (`fn_dump_dblog`). So, for example, we can look at the contents of our second log backup files as shown in Listing 5.16.

```
SELECT  *
FROM    fn_dump_dblog(DEFAULT, DEFAULT, DEFAULT, DEFAULT,
        'C:\SQLBackups\FullRecovery_tail.trn',
                DEFAULT, DEFAULT, DEFAULT, DEFAULT, DEFAULT, DEFAULT,
                DEFAULT, DEFAULT, DEFAULT, DEFAULT, DEFAULT, DEFAULT,
                DEFAULT, DEFAULT, DEFAULT, DEFAULT, DEFAULT, DEFAULT,
                DEFAULT, DEFAULT, DEFAULT, DEFAULT, DEFAULT, DEFAULT,
                DEFAULT, DEFAULT, DEFAULT, DEFAULT, DEFAULT, DEFAULT,
                DEFAULT, DEFAULT, DEFAULT, DEFAULT, DEFAULT, DEFAULT,
                DEFAULT, DEFAULT, DEFAULT, DEFAULT, DEFAULT, DEFAULT,
                DEFAULT, DEFAULT, DEFAULT, DEFAULT, DEFAULT, DEFAULT,
                DEFAULT, DEFAULT, DEFAULT, DEFAULT, DEFAULT, DEFAULT,
                DEFAULT, DEFAULT, DEFAULT, DEFAULT, DEFAULT, DEFAULT,
                DEFAULT, DEFAULT, DEFAULT);
```

Listing 5.16:   Exploring log backups with `fn_dump_dblog`.

It's not pretty and it's unsupported, so use it with caution. It accepts a whole host of parameters, the only one we've defined being the path to the log backup. It returns a vast array of information that we're not going to begin to delve into here, but it does return the **Begin Time** for each of the transactions contained in the file, and it *may* offer some help in working out where to stop a restore operation.

A different technique to point-in-time restores using **STOPAT**, is to try to work out the LSN value associated with, for example, the start of the rogue transaction that deleted your data. We're not going to walk through an LSN-based restore here, but you can find a good explanation of some of the practicalities involved at: HTTP://JANICECLEE.COM/2010/07/25/ALTERNATIVE-TO-RESTORING-TO-A-POINT-IN-TIME/.

An alternative to doing a standby restore is to consider use of a third-party tool such as Red Gate's SQL Virtual Restore (HTTP://WWW.RED-GATE.COM/PRODUCTS/DBA/SQL-VIRTUAL-RESTORE/), which provides a way to mount backups as live, fully functional databases, without a physical restore.

Tail log backups when the database is offline

As discussed earlier, the command BACKUP LOG...WITH NORECOVERY requires that the database is online. If, it's not possible to bring it back online, we can perform an alternative form of the tail log backup, using WITH NO_TRUNCATE.

We can simulate this as shown in Listing 5.17 (first rerun Listings 5.2 to 5.4 to start from a fresh database).

```
USE [master]
GO


ALTER DATABASE [FullRecovery]
SET OFFLINE WITH ROLLBACK IMMEDIATE
GO


/*drop the mdf*/


/* try to bring database online. This will fail but is a necessary step*/
ALTER DATABASE FullRecovery
SET ONLINE
GO
```

```
/*try a NORECOVERY tail log backup */
USE master
GO
BACKUP LOG FullRecovery
TO DISK='D:\SQLBackups\FullRecovery_tail.trn'
WITH INIT, NORECOVERY;
/*Msg 942, Level 14, State 4, Line 1
Database 'FullRecovery' cannot be opened because it is offline.
Msg 3013, Level 16, State 1, Line 1
BACKUP LOG is terminating abnormally.*/

/*A NO_TRUNCATE tail log backup should work */
USE master
GO
BACKUP LOG FullRecovery
TO DISK='D:\SQLBackups\FullRecovery_tail.trn'
WITH INIT, NO_TRUNCATE;
```

Listing 5.17: A tail log backup when the database is offline.

We can then proceed with the restore operation, replacing the existing database, as discussed previously. We'll return to this topic in Chapter 6, when we discuss the BULK_LOGGED recovery model, as there are cases there where this technique won't work.

Summary

In this chapter, we've covered the basics of backing up and restoring log files for databases operating in FULL recovery model, which will be the norm for many production databases.

For most DBAs, the need to perform a point-in-time restore is a rare event, but it's one of those tasks where, if it is necessary, it is critical that it is done, and done well; the DBA's reputation depends on it.

In the case of corruption, drive failure, and so on, point-in-time recovery might, if you're lucky, involve backing up the tail of the transaction log and restoring right to the point of failure. If the transaction log is not available, or if you're restoring in order to revert to some point in time before a "bad transaction" occurred, then the situation becomes trickier, but hopefully some of the techniques covered here will help.

Chapter 6: Managing the Log in BULK_LOGGED Recovery Model

This title is a bit of a misnomer, as we would not generally manage the log, in any long-term sense, by operating a database in the BULK_LOGGED recovery model. However, a DBA may consider switching a database to the BULK_LOGGED recovery model in the short term during, for example, bulk load operations. When a database is operating in the BULK_LOGGED model these, and a few other operations such as index rebuilds, can be **minimally logged** and will therefore use much less space in the log. When rebuilding the clustered index for very large tables, or when bulk loading millions of rows of data, the reduction in log space usage when operating in BULK_LOGGED recovery model, compared to FULL recovery model, can be *very* substantial.

However, we should use BULK_LOGGED recovery only in full knowledge of the implications it has for **database restore and recovery**. For example, it's not possible to restore to a specific point in time within a log backup that contains log records relating to minimally logged operations. Also, there is a special case where a tail log backup will fail if minimally logged operations, recorded while a database was operating in BULK_LOGGED recovery model, exist in the active portion of the transaction log and a data file becomes unavailable as a result of a disaster (such as disk failure).

If your luck is out in terms of the timing of such a disaster, then either of these limitations could lead to data loss. Check the Service Level Agreement (SLA) for the database in question, for acceptable levels of data loss; if it expresses zero tolerance then it's highly unlikely that use of the BULK_LOGGED model, even for short periods, will be acceptable. Conversely, of course, if such a database is subject to regular index rebuilds or bulk loads, then the database owners must understand the implications for log space allocation for that database, of performing these operations under the FULL recovery model.

Having said all this, for many databases, the ability to switch to BULK_LOGGED recovery so that SQL Server will minimally log certain operations, is a very useful weapon in the fight against excessive log growth. In most cases, the SLA will allow enough leeway to make its use acceptable and, with careful planning and procedures, the risks will be minimal.

This chapter will cover:

- what we mean by "minimal logging"

- advantages of minimal logging in terms of log space use

- implications of minimal logging for crash recovery, point-in-time restore, and tail log backups

- best practices for use of BULK_LOGGED recovery.

Minimally Logged Operations

When a database is operating in the FULL recovery model, all operations are fully logged. This means that each log record stores enough information to roll back (undo), or roll forward (redo), the operations that it describes. With all log records in a given log file fully logged, we have a complete description of all the changes made to a database, in that timeframe. This means that, during a restore operation, SQL Server can roll forward through each log record, and then recover the database to the exact state in which it existed at any point in time within that log file.

When a database is operating in BULK_LOGGED (or SIMPLE) recovery model, SQL Server can minimally log certain operations. While some minimally logged operations are obvious (BULK INSERT, bcp or index rebuilds), others are not. For example, INSERT...SELECT can be minimally logged under some circumstances in SQL Server 2008 and later versions.

You can find here a full list of operations that SQL Server can minimally log: HTTP://MSDN.MICROSOFT.COM/EN-US/LIBRARY/MS191244.ASPX. Some of the more common ones are as follows:

- bulk load operations – such as via SSIS, bcp, or BULK INSERT

- SELECT INTO operations

- creating and rebuilding indexes.

It's worth noting that "can be" minimally logged is not the same as "will be" minimally logged. Depending on the indexes that are in place and the plan chosen by the optimizer, SQL Server might still fully log bulk load operations that, in theory, it can minimally log. Due (mainly) to recoverability requirements, SQL Server only minimally logs a bulk data load that is allocating new extents. For example, if we perform a bulk load into a clustered index that already has some data, the load will consist of a mix of adding to pages, splitting pages, and allocating new pages, and so SQL Server can't minimally log. Similarly, it's possible for SQL Server to log minimally inserts into the table, but fully log inserts into the non-clustered indexes. See the white paper, *The Data Loading Performance Guide*, (HTTP://MSDN.MICROSOFT.COM/EN-US/LIBRARY/DD425070.ASPX) for a fuller discussion.

Books Online describes minimally logged operations as "logging only the information that is required to recover the transaction without supporting point-in-time recovery." Similarly, Kalen Delaney, in her book, *SQL Server 2008 Internals* (Chapter 4, page 199), defines minimally logged operations as "ones that log only enough information to roll back the transaction, without supporting point-in-time recovery."

In order to understand the difference between what is logged for a "minimally logged" operation, depending on whether the database uses FULL or BULK_LOGGED recovery, let's try it out and see!

> ### *Data and backup file locations*
>
> *All of the examples in this chapter assume that data and log files are located in* `'D:\SQLData'` *and all backups in* `'D:\SQLBackups'`, *respectively. When running the examples, simply modify these locations as appropriate for your system (and note that, in a real system, we wouldn't store everything on the same drive!).*

We'll use a SELECT...INTO statement, which can be minimally logged in SQL Server 2008, to insert 200 rows, of 2,000 bytes each, into a table called SomeTable. Since the page size in SQL Server is 8 KB, we should get four rows per page and so 50 data pages in all (plus some allocation pages). Listing 6.1 creates a test database, FullRecovery, ensures that it is operating in FULL recovery model, and then runs the SELECT...INTO statement.

```
USE master
GO
IF DB_ID('FullRecovery') IS NOT NULL
    DROP DATABASE FullRecovery;
GO


-- Clear backup history
EXEC msdb.dbo.sp_delete_database_backuphistory
    @database_name = N'FullRecovery'
GO

CREATE DATABASE FullRecovery ON
(NAME = FullRecovery_dat,
  FILENAME = 'D:\SQLData\FullRecovery.mdf'
) LOG ON
(
  NAME = FullRecovery_log,
  FILENAME = 'D:\SQLData\FullRecovery.ldf'
);
ALTER DATABASE FullRecovery SET RECOVERY FULL
GO

USE FullRecovery
GO
```

```
IF OBJECT_ID('dbo.SomeTable', 'U') IS NOT NULL
    DROP TABLE dbo.SomeTable
GO


SELECT TOP ( 200 )
        REPLICATE('a', 2000) AS SomeCol
INTO    SomeTable
FROM    sys.columns AS c;
```

Listing 6.1:   Running a SELECT...INTO operation on a FULL recovery model database.

Now, at this point, we'd like to peek inside the log, and understand what SQL Server recorded in the log because of our fully logged SELECT...INTO statement. There are some third-party log readers for this purpose, but very few of them offer support beyond SQL Server 2005. However, we can use two undocumented and unsupported functions to interrogate the contents of log files (fn_dblog) and log backups (fn_dump_dblog), as shown in Listing 6.2.

```
SELECT  Operation ,
        Context ,
        AllocUnitName ,
   --   Description ,
        [Log Record Length] ,
        [Log Record]
FROM    fn_dblog(NULL, NULL)
```

Listing 6.2:   Investigating log contents using fn_dblog.

Figure 6.1 shows a small portion of the output consisting of a set of eight pages (where the allocation unit is dbo.SomeTable). Notice that the context in each case is LCX_HEAP, so these are the data pages. We also see some allocation pages, in this case a **Differential Changed Map**, tracking extents that have changes since the last database backup (to facilitate differential backups), and some **Page Free Space** (PFS) pages, tracking page allocation and available free space on pages.

	Operation	Context	AllocUnitName	Log Record Length	Log Record
102	LOP_FORMAT_PAGE	LCX_HEAP	dbo.SomeTable	8276	0x0000500090000000480100000100002003C0E00000000010...
103	LOP_SET_BITS	LCX_DIFF_MAP	Unknown Alloc Unit	56	0x00003600000000000000000000000000000000000000000071...
104	LOP_FORMAT_PAGE	LCX_HEAP	dbo.SomeTable	8276	0x0000500090000000480100000A0002003C0E0000000001...
105	LOP_FORMAT_PAGE	LCX_HEAP	dbo.SomeTable	8276	0x0000500090000000480100000C0002003C0E0000000001...
106	LOP_FORMAT_PAGE	LCX_HEAP	dbo.SomeTable	8276	0x0000500090000000480100000D0002003C0E0000000001...
107	LOP_FORMAT_PAGE	LCX_HEAP	dbo.SomeTable	8276	0x0000500090000000480100000E0002003C0E0000000001...
108	LOP_FORMAT_PAGE	LCX_HEAP	dbo.SomeTable	8276	0x0000500090000000480100000F0002003C0E00000000010...
109	LOP_FORMAT_PAGE	LCX_HEAP	dbo.SomeTable	8276	0x00005000900000004801000010002003C0E00000000010...
110	LOP_FORMAT_PAGE	LCX_HEAP	dbo.SomeTable	8276	0x0000500090000000BB0100000100002003C0E0000000001...
111	LOP_SET_FREE_SPACE	LCX_PFS	Unknown Alloc Unit	52	0x00003400000000000000000000000000000000000000A0...
112	LOP_SET_FREE_SPACE	LCX_PFS	Unknown Alloc Unit	52	0x00003400000000000000000000000000000000000000A0...
113	LOP_SET_FREE_SPACE	LCX_PFS	Unknown Alloc Unit	52	0x00003400000000000000000000000000000000000000A0...
114	LOP_SET_FREE_SPACE	LCX_PFS	Unknown Alloc Unit	52	0x00003400000000000000000000000000000000000000A0...
115	LOP_SET_FREE_SPACE	LCX_PFS	Unknown Alloc Unit	52	0x00003400000000000000000000000000000000000000A0...

Figure 6.1: fn_dblog output after SELECT...INTO on a FULL recovery model database.

The log records describing the changes made to SomeTable are all of type LOP_FORMAT_PAGE; they always appear in sets of 8, and each one is 8,276 bytes long. The fact that they appear in sets of 8 indicates that SQL Server was processing the insert one extent at a time and writing one log record for each page. The fact that each one is 8,276 bytes shows that each one contains the image of an entire page, plus log headers. In other words, for the INSERT...INTO command, and others that SQL Server will minimally log in BULK_LOGGED recovery, SQL Server does not log every individual row when run in FULL recovery; rather, it just logs each page image, as it is filled.

A closer examination of the **Log Record** column shows many bytes containing the hex value **0x61**, as shown in Figure 6.2. This translates to decimal 97, which is the ASCII value for 'a', so these are the actual data rows in the log file.

```
0100DB0761616161616161616161616161616161616161616161616161616161616161
00100DB0761616161616161616161616161616161616161616161616161616161616161
00100DB0761616161616161616161616161616161616161616161616161616161616161
00100DB0761616161616161616161616161616161616161616161616161616161616161
00100DB0761616161616161616161616161616161616161616161616161616161616161
00100DB0761616161616161616161616161616161616161616161616161616161616161
00100DB0761616161616161616161616161616161616161616161616161616161616161
```

Figure 6.2: A closer look at the log records.

So in FULL recovery model, SQL Server knows, just by reading the log file, which extents changed and exactly how this affected the contents of the pages. Let's now compare this to the log records that result from performing the same SELECT...INTO operation on a database operating in BULK_LOGGED recovery.

```
USE master
GO
IF DB_ID('BulkLoggedRecovery') IS NOT NULL
    DROP DATABASE BulkLoggedRecovery;
GO

EXEC msdb.dbo.sp_delete_database_backuphistory @database_name =
N'BulkLoggedRecovery'
GO

CREATE DATABASE BulkLoggedRecovery ON
(NAME = BulkLoggedRecovery_dat,
  FILENAME = 'D:\SQLData\BulkLoggedRecovery.mdf'
) LOG ON
(
  NAME = BulkLoggedRecovery_log,
  FILENAME = 'D:\SQLData\BulkLoggedRecovery.ldf'
);
GO

ALTER DATABASE BulkLoggedRecovery SET RECOVERY BULK_LOGGED
GO

BACKUP DATABASE BulkLoggedRecovery TO DISK =
           'D:\SQLBackups\BulkLoggedRecovery.bak'
WITH INIT
GO

USE BulkLoggedRecovery
GO
IF OBJECT_ID('dbo.SomeTable', 'U') IS NOT NULL
    DROP TABLE dbo.SomeTable
GO

SELECT TOP ( 200 )
        REPLICATE('a', 2000) AS SomeCol
INTO    SomeTable
FROM    sys.columns AS c;
```

Listing 6.3: Running a SELECT...INTO operation on a BULK_LOGGED recovery model database.

95

Rerun the `fn_dblog` function, from Listing 6.2, in the `BulkLoggedRecovery` database, and what we get this time is a very different set of log records. There are no `LOP_FORMAT_PAGE` log records at all.

	Operation	Context	AllocUnitName	Log Record Length	Log Record
122	LOP_SET_FREE_SPACE	LCX_PFS	Unknown Alloc Unit	52	0x000003400000000000000000000000000000000000000000A0B01
123	LOP_SET_FREE_SPACE	LCX_PFS	Unknown Alloc Unit	52	0x000003400000000000000000000000000000000000000000A0B01
124	LOP_SET_FREE_SPACE	LCX_PFS	Unknown Alloc Unit	52	0x000003400000000000000000000000000000000000000000A0B01
125	LOP_SET_FREE_SPACE	LCX_PFS	Unknown Alloc Unit	52	0x000003400000000000000000000000000000000000000000A0B01
126	LOP_SET_FREE_SPACE	LCX_PFS	Unknown Alloc Unit	52	0x000003400000000000000000000000000000000000000000A0B01
127	LOP_SET_BITS	LCX_GAM	dbo.SomeTable	60	0x0000360090000000610000003D0002003D0E0000000070802
128	LOP_MODIFY_ROW	LCX_PFS	dbo.SomeTable	88	0x00003E009000000610000059002003D0E00000000040B01
129	LOP_SET_BITS	LCX_IAM	dbo.SomeTable	60	0x0000360090000000610000005A0002003D0E00000000070A5(
130	LOP_SET_BITS	LCX_GAM	dbo.SomeTable	60	0x0000360090000000610000005B0002003D0E0000000070802
131	LOP_MODIFY_ROW	LCX_PFS	dbo.SomeTable	88	0x00003E009000000610000005C0002003D0E00000000040B01
132	LOP_SET_BITS	LCX_IAM	dbo.SomeTable	60	0x0000360090000000610000005D0002003D0E00000000070A5(
133	LOP_SET_BITS	LCX_GAM	dbo.SomeTable	60	0x0000360090000000610000005E0002003D0E0000000070802
134	LOP_MODIFY_ROW	LCX_PFS	dbo.SomeTable	88	0x00003E009000000610000005F0002003D0E00000000040B01
135	LOP_SET_BITS	LCX_IAM	dbo.SomeTable	60	0x0000360090000000610000060002003D0E00000000070A5(
136	LOP_SET_BITS	LCX_DIFF_MAP	Unknown Alloc Unit	56	0x00003600000000000000000000000000000000000000000071806(
137	LOP_SET_FREE_SPACE	LCX_PFS	Unknown Alloc Unit	52	0x000003400000000000000000000000000000000000000000A0B01
138	LOP_SET_FREE_SPACE	LCX_PFS	Unknown Alloc Unit	52	0x000003400000000000000000000000000000000000000000A0B01

Figure 6.3:　`fn_dblog` output after `SELECT...INTO` on a `BULK_LOGGED` database.

This time, the log records for the changes made to `SomeTable` appear in the context of Global Allocation Maps (GAMs) and Index Allocation Maps (IAMs), tracking extent allocation, plus some PFS pages. In other words, SQL Server is logging the extent allocations (and any changes to the metadata, i.e. system tables, which we don't show in Figure 6.3), but the data pages themselves are not there. There is no reference in the log as to what data is on the allocated pages. We do not see here the `0x61` pattern that appeared in the log records for the `FullRecovery` database, and most of the log records are around 100 bytes in size.

Therefore, we now have a clearer picture of exactly what it means for SQL Server to minimally log an operation: it is one where SQL Server logs allocations of the relevant extents, but not the actual content of those extents (i.e. data pages).

The effects of this are twofold. Firstly, it means that SQL Server writes much less information to the transaction log, so the log file will grow at a significantly slower rate than for equivalent operations in the FULL recovery model. It also means that the bulk load operations *may* be faster (but see the later discussion on this topic, in the section on *Advantages of Minimal Logging and BULK_LOGGED Recovery*).

Secondly, however, it means that SQL Server logs only enough information to undo (roll back) the transaction to which the minimally logged operation belongs, but not to redo it (roll it forward). To roll back the transaction containing the SELECT...INTO operation, all SQL Server needs to do is de-allocate the affected pages. Since page allocations are logged, as shown in Figure 6.3, that's possible. To roll the transaction forward is another matter. The log records can be used to re-allocate the pages, but there is no way, when an operation is minimally logged, for SQL Server to use these log records to re-create the contents of the pages.

Minimally logged versus "extent de-allocation only"

For DROP TABLE *and* TRUNCATE TABLE *operations, as for bulk operations, SQL Server logs only the extent de-allocations. However, the former are not true minimally logged operations because their behavior is the same in all recovery models. The behavior of true minimally logged operations is different in* FULL *recovery from in* BULK_LOGGED *(or* SIMPLE*) recovery, in terms of what SQL Server logs. Also, for true minimally logged operations, when log backups are taken, SQL Server captures into the backup file all the data pages affected by a minimally logged operation (we'll discuss this in more detail a little later), for use in restore operations. This does not happen for the* DROP TABLE *and* TRUNCATE TABLE *commands.*

Advantages of Minimal Logging and BULK_LOGGED Recovery

Before we discuss potential issues with use of BULK_LOGGED recovery, let's deal with the major advantages for the DBA.

Operations can be minimally logged in either the SIMPLE or BULK_LOGGED recovery model. However, if we switch a database from FULL to SIMPLE recovery model, we trigger a CHECKPOINT, which truncates the log and we immediately break the LSN chain. No further log backups will be possible until the database is switched back to FULL (or BULK_LOGGED) recovery, and the log chain is restarted with a full database backup, or we "bridge the LSN gap" with a differential database backup.

Switching to BULK_LOGGED from FULL recovery, however, does not break the log chain. It is not necessary to take a database backup after switching the database from FULL recovery to BULK_LOGGED recovery; it's effective immediately. Similarly, it is not necessary to take a database backup when switching back to FULL recovery. However, it is a good idea to take a log backup immediately before switching to BULK_LOGGED and immediately after switching back (see the *Best Practices for Use of BULK_LOGGED* section, later, for further discussion).

Although there are still issues to consider when switching to BULK_LOGGED model, which we'll discuss in detail shortly, it is a much safer option in terms of risk of data loss, since the log chain remains intact. Once the database is working in the BULK_LOGGED model, the real advantage is the reduction in the log space used by operations that can be minimally logged, and the potentially improved performance of these operations.

Let's look at an example of an index rebuild, an operation that can be minimally logged. In FULL recovery model, the index rebuild operation requires log space greater than, or equal to, the size of the table. For large tables, that can cause massive log growth, and this is the root cause of many forum entries from distressed users, along the lines of, "I rebuilt my indexes and my log grew huge / we ran out of disk space!"

In `BULK_LOGGED` recovery, only the page allocations for the new index are logged, so the impact on the transaction log can be substantially less than it would in `FULL` recovery. A similar argument applies to large data loads via bcp or `BULK INSERT`, or for copying data into new tables via `SELECT...INTO` or `INSERT INTO...SELECT`.

To get an idea just how much difference this makes, let's see an example. First, we'll create a table with a clustered index and load it with data (the `Filler` column adds 1,500 bytes per row and ensures we get a table with many pages).

```sql
USE FullRecovery
GO
IF OBJECT_ID('dbo.PrimaryTable_Large', 'U') IS NOT NULL
    DROP TABLE dbo.PrimaryTable_Large
GO
CREATE TABLE PrimaryTable_Large
    (
        ID INT IDENTITY
            PRIMARY KEY ,
        SomeColumn CHAR(4) NULL ,
        Filler CHAR(1500) DEFAULT ''
    );
GO

INSERT  INTO PrimaryTable_Large
        ( SomeColumn
        )
        SELECT TOP 100000
                'abcd '
        FROM    msdb.sys.columns a
                CROSS JOIN msdb.sys.columns b
GO

SELECT  *
FROM    sys.dm_db_index_physical_stats(DB_ID(N'FullRecovery'),
                                    OBJECT_ID(N'PrimaryTable_Large'),
                                    NULL, NULL, 'DETAILED');
```

Listing 6.4:   Creating and loading `PrimaryTable_Large`.

Let's now rebuild the clustered index (consisting of 20,034 pages, according to sys.dm_db_index_physical_stats) in our FULL recovery model database, and see how much log space the index rebuild needs, using with the sys.dm_tran_database_transactions DMV.

```
--truncate the log
USE master
GO
BACKUP LOG FullRecovery
TO DISK = 'D:\SQLBackups\FullRecovery_log.trn'
WITH INIT
GO

-- rebuild index and interrogate log space use, within a transaction
USE FullRecovery
GO
BEGIN TRANSACTION

ALTER INDEX ALL ON dbo.PrimaryTable_Large REBUILD
 -- there's only the clustered index

SELECT  d.name ,
  --      session_id ,
          d.recovery_model_desc ,
  --      database_transaction_begin_time ,
          database_transaction_log_record_count ,
          database_transaction_log_bytes_used ,
          DATEDIFF(ss, database_transaction_begin_time, GETDATE())
                AS SecondsToRebuild
FROM    sys.dm_tran_database_transactions AS dt
        INNER JOIN sys.dm_tran_session_transactions AS st
              ON dt.transaction_id = st.transaction_id
        INNER JOIN sys.databases AS d ON dt.database_id = d.database_id
WHERE d.name = 'FullRecovery'
COMMIT TRANSACTION
```

Listing 6.5: Log space usage when rebuilding a clustered index.

When I ran this code on a database operating in **FULL** recovery, the output from the DMV was as shown in Figure 6.4.

	name	recovery_model_desc	database_transaction_log_record_count	database_transaction_log_bytes_used	Seconds To Rebuild
1	FullRecovery	FULL	20131	166376788	5

Figure 6.4: Index rebuild time and log space use in **FULL** recovery.

It took approximately 5 seconds to rebuild the index, and the rebuilds required about 166 MB of log space for 20,131 log records; this is ignoring the log reservation in case of rollback, so the total log space required is larger.

If we run the same example in the **BulkLoggedRecovery** database, the output is as shown in Figure 6.5.

	name	recovery_model_desc	database_transaction_log_record_count	database_transaction_log_bytes_used	Seconds To Rebuild
1	BulkLoggedRecovery	BULK_LOGGED	131	589908	4

Figure 6.5: Index rebuild time and log space use in BULK_LOGGED recovery.

The rebuild appears to be a bit faster, at 4 seconds; however, because the index in this example is quite small, and because the data and log files are both on a single drive, not much can be concluded from that time difference. The main point here is the difference in the log space used. In **BULK_LOGGED** recovery, that index rebuild only used about 0.6 MB of log space, compared to the 166 MB of log space in **FULL** recovery. That's a major saving considering that this was quite a small table, at only 160 MB in size.

In case anyone's wondering whether the behavior will be any different in **SIMPLE** recovery, look at Figure 6.6 (the code to reproduce the example in a **SIMPLE** recovery database, as well as **BULK_LOGGED**, is included in the code download for this chapter).

name	recovery_model_desc	database_transaction_log_record_count	database_transaction_log_bytes_used	SecondsToRebuild
1 SimpleRecovery	SIMPLE	131	589908	4

Figure 6.6:   Index rebuild time and log space use in SIMPLE recovery.

As expected, the behavior is the same as for BULK_LOGGED recovery, since operations that are minimally logged in BULK_LOGGED recovery are also minimally logged in SIMPLE recovery.

This is the major reason for running a database in BULK_LOGGED recovery; it offers both the database recovery options of FULL recovery (mostly, see the coming sections), but it reduces the amount of log space used by certain operations, in the same way as SIMPLE recovery. Note also, that if the database is a log-shipping primary, we cannot switch the database into SIMPLE recovery for index rebuilds without having to redo the log shipping afterwards, but we can switch it to BULK_LOGGED for the index rebuilds.

Finally, note that database mirroring requires FULL recovery only and, as such, a database that is a database mirroring principal cannot use BULK_LOGGED recovery.

Implications of Minimally Logged Operations

Earlier, we discussed how, when a database is operating in BULK_LOGGED recovery, the log contains only the extent allocations (plus metadata), and not the actual results of the minimally logged operation (i.e. not, for example, the actual data that was inserted). This means that the log on its own only holds enough information to roll back a transaction, not to redo it. In order to perform the latter, SQL Server needs to read the log's records describing the operation *and* the actual data pages affected by the operation.

This has implications whenever SQL Server needs to redo transactions, namely during **crash recovery**, and during database **restore** operations. It also has implications for **log backup operations**, both in terms of what SQL Server must copy into the backup file, and the situations in which this may or may not be possible.

Crash recovery

Crash recovery, also called restart recovery, is a process that SQL Server performs whenever it brings a database online. So for example, if a database does not shut down cleanly, then upon restart SQL Server goes through the database's transaction log. It undoes any transaction that had not committed at the time of the shutdown and redoes any transaction that had committed but whose changes had not been persisted to disk.

This is possible because, as discussed in Chapter 1, the **Write Ahead Logging** mechanism ensures that the log records associated with a data modification are written to disk before either the transaction commits or the data modification is written to disk, whichever happens first. SQL Server can write the changes to the data file at any time, before the transaction commits or after, via the checkpoint or Lazy Writer. Hence, for normal operations (i.e. ones that are fully logged), SQL Server has sufficient information in the transaction log to tell whether an operation needs to be undone or redone, and has sufficient information to roll forward or roll back.

For operations that were minimally logged, however, roll forward is not possible as there's not enough information in the log. Therefore, when dealing with minimally logged operations in SIMPLE or BULK_LOGGED recovery model, another process, **Eager Write**, guarantees that the thread that is executing the bulk operation hardens to disk any extents modified by the minimally logged operation, before the transaction is complete. This is in contrast to normal operations where only the log records have to be hardened before the transaction is complete, and the data pages are written later by a system process (Lazy Writer or checkpoint).

This means that crash recovery will never have to redo a minimally logged operation since SQL Server guarantees that the modified data pages will be on disk at the time the transaction commits, and hence the minimal logging has no effect on the crash recovery process.

One side effect of this requirement that SQL Server writes both log records and modified data pages to disk before the transaction commits, is that it may actually result in the minimally logged operation being *slower* than a regular transaction, if the data file is not able to handle the large volume of writes. Minimally logged operations are usually faster than normal operations, but there is no guarantee. The only guarantee is that they write *less* information to the transaction log.

Database restores

SQL Server also needs to perform redo operations when restoring full, differential, or log backups. As we've discussed, for a minimally logged operation the affected pages are on disk at the point the transaction completes and so SQL Server simply copies those pages into any full or differential backup files, and restores from these backups are unaffected.

Restores from log backups, however, are more interesting. If the log backup only contained the log records relating to extent allocation, then on restoring the log backup there would be no way to re-create the contents of the extents that the minimally logged operation affected. This is because, as we saw earlier, the log does not contain the inserted data, just the extent allocations and metadata.

In order to enable log restores when there are minimally logged operations, included in the log backup are not just the log records, but also the images of any extent (set of eight pages) affected by the minimally logged operation. This *doesn't* mean images of them as they were after the minimally logged operation, but the pages as they are at the time of the log backup. SQL Server maintains a bitmap allocation page, called the **ML map** or **bulk-logged change map**, with a bit for every extent. Any extents affected by the minimally logged operation have their bit set to 1. The log backup operation reads this page and so knows exactly what extents to include in the backup. That log backup will then clear the ML map.

So, for example, let's say we have a timeline like that shown in Figure 6.7, where a log backup occurs at 10:00, then at (1) a minimally logged operation (let's say a **BULK INSERT**) affected pages 1308–1315 among others, at (2) an **UPDATE** affected pages 1310 and 1311 and at (3) another log backup occurred.

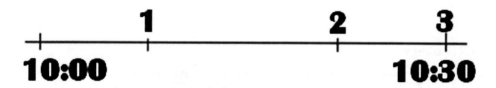

Figure 6.7:   Example timeline for database operations and log backups.

The log backup at 10:30 backs up the log records covering the period 10:00–10:30. Since there was a minimally logged operation within that log interval, it copies the extents affected by the minimally logged operations into the log backup. It copies them as they appear at the time of the log backup, so they will reflect the effects of the **BULK INSERT** and the **UPDATE**, plus any further modifications that may have taken place between the **UPDATE** and the log backup.

This affects how we can restore the log. It also affects the size of the log backups and, under certain circumstances, may affect tail log backups, but we'll get to that in more detail in the next section.

Let's take a look an example of how minimally logged operations can affect a point-in-time restore. Figure 6.8 depicts an identical backup timeline for two databases. The green bar represents a full database backup and the yellow bars represent a series of log backups. The only difference between the two databases is that the first is operating in **FULL** recovery model, and the second in **BULK LOGGED**.

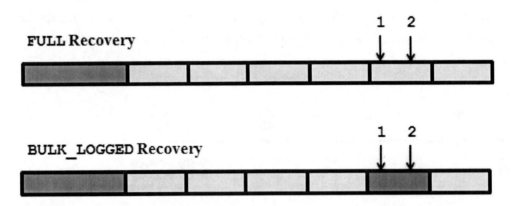

Figure 6.8:   Database backup timeline.

The time span of the fifth log backup is 10:00 to 10:30. At 10:10, a BULK INSERT command (1) loaded a set of data. This bulk data load completed without a hitch but, in an unrelated incident at 10:20, a user ran a "rogue" data modification (2) and crucial data was lost. The project manager informs the DBA team and requests that they restore the database to a point in time just before the transaction that resulted in data loss started, at 10:20.

In the FULL recovery model database, this is not an issue. The bulk data load was fully logged and we can restore the database to any point in time within that log file. We simply restore the last full database backup, without recovery, and apply the log files to the point in time right before the unfortunate data loss incident occurred, using the RESTORE LOG command with the STOPAT parameter, to stop the restore operation sometime before 10:20.

In the BULK_LOGGED database, we have a problem. We can restore to any point in time within the first four log backups, but not to any point in time within the fifth log backup, which contains the minimally logged operations. Remember that for this log backup we only have the extents affected by the minimally logged operation, as they existed at the time of the log backup. The restore of the fifth log backup is "all or nothing:" either we apply none of the operations in this log file, stopping the restore at the end of the fourth file, or we apply all of them, restoring to the end of the file, or proceeding to restore to any point in time within the sixth log backup.

If we tried to restore that fifth log backup, with STOPAT 10:15 (a time between the minimally logged operation and the rogue modification), SQL is not going to walk the rest of the log backup figuring out what operations it needs to undo on the pages that were affected by the minimally logged operation. It has a simpler reaction:

```
Msg 4341, Level 16, State 1, Line 2
This log backup contains bulk-logged changes. It cannot be used to stop at an arbitrary point
in time.
```

Unfortunately, if we apply the whole of the fifth log file backup, this would defeat the purpose of the recovery, since the errant process committed its changes somewhere inside of that log backup file, so we'd simply be removing the data we were trying to get back! We have little choice but to restore up to the end of the fourth log, recover the database, and report the loss of any data changes made after this time.

This inability to restore the database to point-in-time if there are minimally logged operations within the log interval is something that must be considered when choosing to run a database in BULK_LOGGED recovery, either for short or long periods. It is easy to identify whether or not a specific log backup contains any minimally logged operations. A RESTORE HEADERONLY returns a set of details about the backup in question, including a column HasBulkLoggedData. In addition, the msdb backupset table has a column, has_bulk_logged_data. If the column value is 1, then the log backup contains minimally logged operations and can only be restored entirely or not at all. That said, finding this out while planning or executing a restore may be an unpleasant surprise.

Log backup size

The need to copy into the log backup the pages affected by a minimally logged operation affects the size of log backups. Essentially, it means that while the actual log will grow less for a bulk operation in a BULK_LOGGED recovery database, compared to a FULL recovery database, the log backup sizes will not be smaller, and may occasionally be bigger than the comparable log backups for FULL recovery databases.

To see the possible impact of minimally logged operations, and BULK_LOGGED recovery model on the size of the log backups, we'll look at a simple example. First, rerun the portion of Listing 6.3 that drops and re-creates the BulkLoggedRecovery database, sets the recovery model to BULK_LOGGED and then takes a full database backup. Next, run Listing 6.6 to create 500K rows in SomeTable.

```
USE BulkLoggedRecovery
GO
IF OBJECT_ID('dbo.SomeTable', 'U') IS NOT NULL
    DROP TABLE dbo.SomeTable ;
SELECT TOP 500000
        SomeCol = REPLICATE('a', 2000)
INTO    dbo.SomeTable
FROM    sys.all_columns ac1
        CROSS JOIN sys.all_columns ac2 ;
GO
```

Listing 6.6:   Insert 500K rows into SomeTable in the BulkLoggedRecovery database.

Next, we check current log space usage, and then back up the log.

```
DBCC SQLPERF(LOGSPACE) ;
--24 MB


--truncate the log
USE master


GO
BACKUP LOG BulkLoggedRecovery
TO DISK = 'D:\SQLBackups\BulkLoggedRecovery_log.trn'
WITH INIT
GO
```

Listing 6.7:   Backing up the log for `BulkLoggedRecovery`.

Given that the log size is only about 24 MB, you may be surprised to see the size of the log backup, about 1 GB in my test! For a database in FULL recovery, you'll find that the log size and log backup size are both about 1 GB.

Tail log backups

Let's imagine that a hardware glitch causes some data corruption, but the database is still online, and we wish to restore over that database. Performing a tail log backup, with BACKUP LOG...WITH NORECOVERY, will capture the remaining contents of the log file and put the database into a restoring state, so that no further transactions against that database will succeed, and we can begin the restore operation. This sort of **tail log backup**, as well as normal log backups, requires the database to be online (so that SQL Server can stamp information regarding the log backup into the database header).

However, assume instead that the damage to the data file is severe enough that the database becomes unavailable and an attempt to bring it back online fails. If the database is in FULL recovery model, with regular log backups, then as long as the log file is still available, we can take a tail log backup, but using the NO_TRUNCATE option instead, i.e. BACKUP LOG...WITH NO_TRUNCATE. This operation backs up the log file without truncating it and doesn't require the database to be online.

With the existing backups (full, perhaps differential, and then log) and the tail log backup, we can restore the database up to the exact point that it failed. We can do that because the log contains sufficient information to re-create all of the committed transactions.

However, if the database is in BULK_LOGGED recovery and there are minimally logged operations in the active portion of the transaction log, then the log does not contain sufficient information to re-create all of the committed transactions, and the actual data pages are required to be available when we take the tail log backup. If the data file is not available, then that log backup cannot copy the data pages it needs to restore a consistent database. Let's see this in action, using the BulkLoggedRecovery database.

```
BACKUP DATABASE BulkLoggedRecovery
    TO DISK = 'D:\SQLBackups\BulkLoggedRecovery2.bak'
WITH INIT
GO
USE BulkLoggedRecovery
GO

IF OBJECT_ID('dbo.SomeTable', 'U') IS NOT NULL
    DROP TABLE dbo.SomeTable ;
SELECT TOP 200
        SomeCol = REPLICATE('a', 2000)
    INTO    dbo.SomeTable
    FROM    sys.all_columns ac1
GO

SHUTDOWN WITH NOWAIT
```

Listing 6.8: Create the BulkLoggedRecovery database, perform a SELECT INTO, and then shut down.

With the SQL Server service shut down, go to the data folder and delete the **mdf** file for the BulkLoggedRecovery database, and then restart SQL Server. It's not a complete simulation of a drive failure, but it's close enough for the purposes of this demo.

When SQL Server restarts, the database is not available, which is no surprise since its primary data file is missing. The state is `Recovery_Pending`, meaning that SQL couldn't open the database to run crash recovery on it.

```
USE master
GO
SELECT  name ,
        state_desc
FROM    sys.databases
WHERE   name = 'BulkLoggedRecovery'


name                            state_desc
-----------------------------------------------
BulkLoggedRecovery        RECOVERY_PENDING
```

Listing 6.9: The `BulkLoggedRecovery` database is in a `Recovery_Pending` state.

In Listing 6.10, we attempt to take a tail log backup (note that NO_TRUNCATE implies COPY_ONLY and CONTINUE_AFTER_ERROR):

```
BACKUP LOG BulkLoggedRecovery
TO DISK = 'D:\SQLBackups\BulkLoggedRecovery_tail.trn'
WITH NO_TRUNCATE

Processed 7 pages for database 'BulkLoggedRecovery', file 'BulkLoggedRecovery_log' on file 1.
BACKUP WITH CONTINUE_AFTER_ERROR successfully generated a backup of the damaged database.
Refer to the SQL Server error log for information about the errors that were encountered.
BACKUP LOG successfully processed 7 pages in 0.007 seconds (7.463 MB/sec).
```

Listing 6.10: Attempting a tail log backup using BACKUP LOG...WITH NO_TRUNCATE.

Well, it said that it succeeded (and despite the warning, there were no errors in the error log). Now, let's try to restore this database, as shown in Listing 6.11.

```
RESTORE DATABASE BulkLoggedRecovery
FROM DISK = 'D:\SQLBackups\BulkLoggedRecovery2.bak'
WITH NORECOVERY

RESTORE LOG BulkLoggedRecovery
FROM DISK = 'D:\SQLBackups\BulkLoggedRecovery_tail.trn'
WITH RECOVERY


Processed 184 pages for database 'BulkLoggedRecovery', file 'BulkLoggedRecovery' on file 1.
Processed 3 pages for database 'BulkLoggedRecovery', file 'BulkLoggedRecovery_log' on file 1.
RESTORE DATABASE successfully processed 187 pages in 0.043 seconds (33.895 MB/sec).

Msg 3182, Level 16, State 2, Line 5
The backup set cannot be restored because the database was damaged when the backup occurred.
Salvage attempts may exploit WITH CONTINUE_AFTER_ERROR.
Msg 3013, Level 16, State 1, Line 5
RESTORE LOG is terminating abnormally.
```

Listing 6.11: Attempting to restore BulkLoggedRecovery.

Well, that didn't work. Let's follow the advice of the error message and see if we can restore the log using CONTINUE_AFTER_ERROR.

```
RESTORE DATABASE BulkLoggedRecovery
FROM DISK = 'D:\SQLBackups\BulkLoggedRecovery2.bak'
WITH NORECOVERY

RESTORE LOG BulkLoggedRecovery
FROM DISK = 'D:\SQLBackups\BulkLoggedRecovery_tail.trn'
WITH RECOVERY, CONTINUE_AFTER_ERROR

Processed 184 pages for database 'BulkLoggedRecovery', file 'BulkLoggedRecovery' on file 1.
Processed 3 pages for database 'BulkLoggedRecovery', file 'BulkLoggedRecovery_log' on file 1.
RESTORE DATABASE successfully processed 187 pages in 0.037 seconds (39.392 MB/sec).
Processed 0 pages for database 'BulkLoggedRecovery', file 'BulkLoggedRecovery' on file 1.
Processed 7 pages for database 'BulkLoggedRecovery', file 'BulkLoggedRecovery_log' on file 1.
The backup set was written with damaged data by a BACKUP WITH CONTINUE_AFTER_ERROR.
RESTORE WITH CONTINUE_AFTER_ERROR was successful but some damage was encountered.
Inconsistencies in the database are possible.
RESTORE LOG successfully processed 7 pages in 0.013 seconds (4.018 MB/sec).
```

Listing 6.12: Restoring the log backup using CONTINUE_AFTER_ERROR.

That worked, so let's investigate the state of the restored database. Rerun Listing 6.9 and you'll see it's reported as ONLINE, and SomeTable, the target of SELECT...INTO exists, so let's see if any of the data made it into the table (remember, the page allocations were logged, the contents of the pages were not).

```
USE BulkLoggedRecovery
GO
IF OBJECT_ID('dbo.SomeTable', 'U') IS NOT NULL
    PRINT 'SomeTable exists'

SELECT  *
FROM    SomeTable

Msg 824, Level 24, State 2, Line 1
SQL Server detected a logical consistency-based I/O error: incorrect pageid (expected
1:184; actual 0:0). It occurred during a read of page (1:184) in database ID 32 at offset
0x00000000170000 in file 'C:\Program Files\Microsoft SQL Server\MSSQL10.MSSQLSERVER\MSSQL\
DATA\BulkLoggedRecovery.mdf'. Additional messages in the SQL Server error log or system
event log may provide more detail. This is a severe error condition that threatens database
integrity and must be corrected immediately. Complete a full database consistency check (DBCC
CHECKDB). This error can be caused by many factors; for more information, see SQL Server
Books Online.
```

Listing 6.13:   Attempting to read SomeTable.

Note that this was the error message from SQL Server 2008 Enterprise Edition. It's possible you'll see different errors on other versions. In any event, this doesn't look good; let's see what DBCC CHECKDB says about the state of the database.

```
DBCC CHECKDB ('BulkLoggedRecovery') WITH NO_INFOMSGS, ALL_ERRORMSGS

Msg 8921, Level 16, State 1, Line 1
Check terminated. A failure was detected while collecting facts. Possibly tempdb out of space
or a system table is inconsistent. Check previous errors.
```

Listing 6.14:   Checking the state of BulkLoggedRecovery with DBCC CHECKDB.

This doesn't look good at all, unfortunately (and TempDB was not out of space). About the only sensible option here is to restore again and leave off the tail log backup. It means that any transactions that committed between the last normal log backup and the point of failure are lost.

This is another important consideration when deciding to run a database in BULK_LOGGED recovery model for long or short periods. In FULL recovery model, a tail log backup requires access only to the transaction log. Therefore, we can still back up the transaction log even if the MDF files are unavailable, due to disk failure, for example. However, in BULK_LOGGED model, if any minimally logged operations have occurred since the last log backup, it will mean that we cannot perform a tail log backup, if the data files containing the data affected by the minimally logged operations become unavailable. The reason for this is that when performing a transaction log backup in BULK_LOGGED model, SQL Server has to back up to the transaction log backup file all the actual extents (i.e. the data) that the bulk operation modified, as well as the transaction log entries. In other words, SQL Server needs access to the data files in order to do the tail log backup.

Best Practices for Use of BULK_LOGGED

Firstly, check the SLA for the database is question for the acceptable risk of data loss. If no data loss is acceptable, then plan to perform all operations in FULL recovery model, with the implications this has for log growth. If you can complete the operations you wish to minimally log within the maximum allowable data loss, as specified in the SLA, then you can consider using BULK_LOGGED recovery.

The golden rule, when using the BULK_LOGGED recovery model is to use it for as short a time as possible and to try, as far as possible, to isolate the minimally logged operations into their own log backup. Therefore, take a transaction log backup immediately prior to switching to BULK_LOGGED recovery and another transaction log backup immediately upon switching back to FULL recovery. This will ensure that the smallest possible of time and smallest number of transactions are within a log interval that contains minimally logged operations.

To illustrate how this reduces risk, consider the following scenario:

- 1:00 a.m. Full backup

- 1:15 a.m. Transaction log backup1

- 2:15 a.m. Transaction log backup2

- 2:40 a.m. Switch to **BULK_LOGGED**, Bulk operation begins

- 3:05 a.m. Bulk operation ends

- 3:10 a.m. – **FAILURE** – MDF becomes unavailable

- 3:15 a.m. Transaction log backup3

In this case, the 3.15 a.m. log backup would fail, as would a subsequent attempt to do a tail log backup. All we could do is restore the full backup followed by the first two log backups, so we would lose 55 minutes-worth of data.

If instead, we had adopted the following regime, we would have been in a much better situation:

- 1:00 a.m. Full backup

- 1:15 a.m. Transaction log backup1

- 2:15 a.m. Transaction log backup2

- 2:35 a.m. Transaction log backup3

- 2:40 a.m. Switch to **BULK_LOGGED**, Bulk operation begins

- 3:05 a.m. Bulk operation ends

- 3:05 a.m. Switch back to **FULL** and perform transaction log backup4

- 3:10 a.m. – **FAILURE** – MDF becomes unavailable

- 3:15 a.m. Transaction log backup5

Here, the 3:15 log backup would also fail, but we would subsequently be able to perform a tail log backup, since log backup4 ensures that there are no minimally logged operations in the live log. We could then restore the full backup, the four transaction log backups, and the tail log backup to recover to the point of failure at 3.15 a.m.

Even given these precautionary log backups, it is best to perform any minimally logged operations out of hourse, when very few, if any, other transactions are being performed. This way, if anything goes wrong we may simply be able replay the bulk load to restore the data.

Even if you minimize risk by taking extra log backups before and after every bulk operation, it is inadvisable to operate a database continually in BULK_LOGGED model. It can be very hard, depending on your environment, to exert total control over who might perform a minimally logged operation, and when. Bear in mind that any table owner can create or rebuild indexes on that table; anyone who can create a table can also run SELECT...INTO statements.

Finally, we recommend reading *The Data Loading Performance Guide* (HTTP://MSDN. MICROSOFT.COM/EN-US/LIBRARY/DD425070.ASPX), which offers a lot of advice on achieving high-speed bulk data modifications, and discusses how to measure the potential benefit that will arise from minimal logging, using Trace Flag 610.

Summary

The BULK_LOGGED recovery model offers a way to perform data loads and some database maintenance operations such as index rebuilds without the transaction log overhead that they would normally have in FULL recovery model, but while still keeping the log chain intact. The downsides of this include greater potential data loss if a disaster occurs during, or over the same time span as, the bulk operation. In other words, you won't be able to use the STOPAT option when restoring a log file that contains minimally logged operations. It is still possible to restore the entire transaction log backup to roll the database forward, and it is still possible to restore to a point in time in a subsequent log file which doesn't contain any minimally logged operations. However, in the event of an application bug, or a user change that causes data to be deleted, around the same period as the minimally logged operation, it will not be possible to stop at a specific point in time in the log in which these changes are recorded, in order to recover the data that was deleted.

When using **BULK_LOGGED** recovery, keep in mind the increased risks of data loss, and use the recovery model only for the duration of the maintenance or data load operations and not as a default recovery model.

Even with the increased risks, it is a viable and useful option and is something that DBAs should consider when planning data loads or index maintenance.

Acknowledgements

Many thanks to Shawn McGehee, author of *SQL Server Backup and Restore* (HTTP://WWW.SIMPLE-TALK.COM/BOOKS/SQL-BOOKS/SQL-BACKUP-AND-RESTORE/) for contributing additional material to the *Database restores* section of this chapter.

Chapter 7: Dealing with Excessive Log Growth

This chapter will examine the most common problems and forms of mismanagement that lead to excessive growth of the transaction log, including:

- operating a database in FULL recovery model, without taking log backups

- performing index maintenance

- long-running or uncommitted transactions that prevent space in the transaction log from being reused.

Of course, if growth is left unchecked, the log file may expand until it devours all of the available disk space or the maximum size specified for the log file, at which point you'll receive the infamous 9002 (transaction log full) error, and the database will become read-only. This chapter will cover the correct ways to respond to runaway log growth and the 9002 error, and also explain why commonly given advice to truncate the log and shrink it is often dangerous.

Finally, we'll cover strategies for ensuring smooth and predictable growth of your log file, while minimizing problems associated with log fragmentation. In a busy database, a large transaction log may be a simple fact of life and, managed properly, this is not necessarily a bad thing, even if the log file space is unused a majority of the time.

Sizing and Growing the Log

Whenever a log file needs to grow, and additional space is allocated, this space is divided evenly into VLFs, based on the amount of space that is being allocated.

For example, the log file may, by default, have an initial size of 2 MB and a ten percent auto-growth increment (settings inherited from the `model` database). This means that, initially at least, the log file will grow in very small increments and so have a large number of small VLFs.

When we allocate additional space in very large chunks, for example when initially sizing the log to 16 GB in a single operation, the resulting transaction log has a small number of larger VLFs.

A very high number of small VLFs, a condition referred to as log file fragmentation, can have a considerable impact on performance, especially for crash recovery, restores, and backups, particularly log backups. In other words, it can affect the performance of operations that read the log file. We will examine this problem in more detail in Chapter 8.

Transaction log VLFs – too many or too few?

*SQL Server MVP Kimberly Tripp discusses the impact of VLF sizes and provides guidance for how to properly manage VLF size in her blog post, Transaction Log VLFs – too many or too few? (*HTTP://WWW. SQLSKILLS.COM/BLOGS/KIMBERLY/POST/TRANSACTION-LOG-VLFS-TOO-MANY-OR-TOO-FEW.ASPX*).*

Conversely, if the log file has only a few VLFs that are very large, we risk tying up large portions of the log for long periods. Each VLF will hold a very large number of log records, and SQL Server cannot truncate a VLF until it contains no part of the active log. In cases where truncation is delayed for some reason (see the *Lack of log space reuse* section), this can lead to rapid log growth. For example, let's assume that each VLF is 1 GB in size and that the log is full. You perform a log backup, but all VLFs contain some part of the active log and so SQL Server cannot truncate the log. It has no option but to add more VLFs and, if the growth increment for the log is set to a similarly large size then the log might grow rapidly, until some existing VLFs become eligible for truncation.

As such, it's important that we size the log appropriately initially, and then grow it in appropriately sized steps, to minimize log fragmentation but also to avoid rapid growth.

There is also a second reason why it is very important to size the log appropriately and grow it in a very controlled fashion: for log files, each growth event is a relatively expensive operation. It is natural that both data and log files will grow in size over time. SQL Server can optimize the process of adding new data files and expanding existing data files, via **instant file initialization** (introduced in SQL Server 2005, this allows the data files to allocate space on disk without having to fill the space with zeros). Unfortunately, the same is not true for log files, which still require initialization and "zeroing out" whenever space is allocated for log file creation or growth.

> *Why can't the transaction log use instant initialization?*
>
> *For further information about transaction log zeroing, see Paul Randal's blog post, Search Engine Q&A #24: Why can't the transaction log use instant initialization? (*HTTP://SQLSKILLS.COM/ BLOGS/PAUL/POST/SEARCH-ENGINE-QA-24-WHY-CANT-THE-TRANSACTION-LOG-USE-INSTANT- INITIALIZATION.ASPX*).*

Diagnosing a Runaway Transaction Log

If you are experiencing uncontrolled growth of the transaction log, it is due, either to a very high rate of log activity, or to factors that are preventing space in the log file from being reused, or both.

If the growth is due primarily to excessive log activity, you need to investigate whether there might be log activity that could be avoided, for example by adjusting how you carry out bulk data and index maintenance operations, so that these operations are not fully logged (i.e. the BULK_LOGGED recovery model is used for these operations). However, any bulk-logged operation will immediately prevent point-in-time recovery to any point within a log backup that contains records relating to the minimally logged operations (refer to Chapter 6 for full details). If this is not acceptable, you must simply accept a large log as a fact, and plan its growth and management (such as frequency of log backups) accordingly, as described in the *Proper Log Management* section, later in this chapter.

If the growth is due to a lack of log space reuse, you need to find out what is preventing this reuse and take steps to correct the issue.

Excessive logging: index maintenance operations

Index maintenance operations are a very common cause of excessive transaction log usage and growth, especially in databases using the FULL recovery model. The amount of log space required to perform index maintenance depends on the following factors:

- **Rebuild or reorganize** – Index rebuilds generally use a lot more space in the log.

- **Recovery model** – If the risks to point-in-time recovery are understood and acceptable, then index rebuilds can be minimally logged by temporarily switching the database to run in BULK LOGGED recovery model. Index reorganization, however, is always fully logged.

Index rebuilds

Rebuilding an index offline, using ALTER INDEX REBUILD (or the deprecated
DBCC DBREINDEX in SQL Server 2000) drops the target index and rebuilds it from
scratch (online index rebuilds do not drop the existing index until the end of the
rebuild operation).

Logging and online index rebuilds

*Online index rebuild is a fully logged operation on SQL Server 2008 and later, whereas it is minimally
logged in SQL Server 2005. Therefore, performing such operations in later SQL Server versions will
require substantially more transaction log space. See:* HTTP://SUPPORT.MICROSOFT.COM/KB/2407439,
as well as Kalen Delaney's blog, investigating logging during online and offline index rebuilds, for both
FULL *and* BULK_LOGGED *recovery model databases:* HTTP://SQLBLOG.COM/BLOGS/KALEN_DELANEY/
ARCHIVE/2011/03/08/WHAT-GETS-LOGGED-FOR-INDEX-REBUILDS.ASPX.

In the FULL recovery model, index rebuilds can be a very resource-intensive operation,
requiring a lot of space in the transaction log. In the SIMPLE or BULK_LOGGED recovery
model, rebuilding an index is a minimally logged operation, meaning that only the allocations are logged, and the actual pages are not changed, therefore reducing the amount of
log space required by the operation.

If you switch to the SIMPLE model to perform an index rebuild, the LSN chain
will be immediately broken. You'll only be able to recover your database to a point
in time contained in the previous transaction log backup. To restart the chain, you'll
need to switch back to the FULL model and immediately take a full or differential
database backup.

If you switch to the BULK_LOGGED model (see Chapter 6), the LSN chain is always
maintained but there are still implications for your ability to perform point-in-time
restores, since a log backup that contains a minimally logged operation can't be used to
recover to a point in time. If the ability to perform a point-in-time recovery is paramount

for a database, then don't use the BULK_LOGGED recovery model for index rebuilds or any other minimally logged operation, unless you can do it at a time when there is no concurrent user activity in the database. Alternatively, consider performing index reorganizations, in FULL recovery model, where possible.

If the BULK_LOGGED model is used, take steps to minimize the time period where point-in-time restore is unavailable, and so minimize exposure to data loss. To do this, take a log backup in FULL model, switch to BULK_LOGGED, perform the index rebuild, then switch back to FULL and take another log backup.

A final important point to note is that an ALTER INDEX REBUILD operation occurs in a *single* transaction. If the index is large, this could represent a long-running transaction that will prevent space reuse in the log for its duration. This means that, even if you rebuild an index in SIMPLE model, where you might think that the log should remain small since it is auto-truncated after a CHECKPOINT operation, and the rebuild is minimally logged, the log file can still expand quite rapidly during an extensive rebuild operation.

Index reorganization

In contrast to rebuilding an index, reorganizing (defragmenting) an index, using ALTER INDEX REORGANIZE or, in SQL Server 2000, DBCC INDEXDEFRAG (since deprecated) is always a fully logged operation, regardless of the recovery model, and so the actual page changes are always logged. However, index reorganizations generally require less log space than an index rebuild, although this is a function of the degree of fragmentation in the index; a heavily fragmented index will require more log space to reorganize than a minimally fragmented one.

Furthermore, the ALTER INDEX REORGANIZE operation is accomplished using multiple shorter transactions. Therefore, when performed in conjunction with frequent log backups (or when working in SIMPLE model), log space can be made available for reuse *during* the operation, so minimizing the size requirements for the transaction log during the operation.

For example, rebuilding a 20 GB index can require more than 20 GB of space for the rebuild operation because it occurs in a single transaction. However, reorganizing a 20 GB index may require much less log space because each page allocation change in the reorganization is a separate transaction, and so the log records can be truncated with frequent log backups, allowing the log space to be reused.

Strategies for controlling excessive logging

If your organization has zero tolerance to any potential data loss, then you'll have no choice but to run all database maintenance operations in the FULL recovery model, and plan your log size and growth appropriately. Since index rebuilds occur as a single transaction, the log will be at least as large as the largest index that you are rebuilding. As discussed above, index reorganizations require less log space, and allow for log truncation via log backups, during the operation. As such, they may offer a viable alternative to rebuilds, while avoiding explosive log growth.

If your SLAs and Operational Level Agreements (OLAs) allow some potential for data loss, then switching to BULK_LOGGED recovery at the start of an index rebuild can minimize the amount of space required to rebuild the index. However, do so in a way that minimizes exposure to data loss, as discussed earlier.

Regardless of the recovery model in use, you can minimize the impact of index maintenance operations on the transaction log by reorganizing rather than rebuilding, if possible. Microsoft has provided guidelines appropriate for most, but not all, environments for determining when to rebuild an index versus when to reorganize it to minimize the impact of index maintenance operations (see *Reorganize and Rebuild Indexes*, HTTP://TECHNET.MICROSOFT.COM/EN-US/LIBRARY/MS189858.ASPX). They state that for fragmentation levels greater than 5 percent but less than or equal to 30 percent, you should reorganize the index, and for fragmentation levels greater than 30 percent, you should rebuild it.

However, the most effective weapon in guarding against excessive log growth during index maintenance is to maintain only those indexes that really need it. With the SSMS Maintenance Plans Wizard, index maintenance is an all-or-nothing process: you either rebuild (or reorganize) all indexes in your database (and all databases in the maintenance plan) or you maintain none of them. A better approach is to use the `sys.dm_db_index_physical_stats` DMV to investigate fragmentation and so determine a rebuild/reorganize strategy based on need.

Ola Hallengren's free maintenance scripts

Ola Hallengren offers a comprehensive set of free maintenance scripts which demonstrate how to use `sys.dm_db_index_physical_stats` *to perform index analysis for intelligent maintenance, and which can be used as a replacement for Database Maintenance Plans created by the wizards in SSMS* (HTTP://OLA.HALLENGREN.COM).

The best approach, however, is to schedule regular maintenance on only those indexes where you can prove a positive, sustained impact on query performance. Logical fragmentation (index pages in the wrong order) thwarts SQL Server's read-ahead mechanism (HTTP://MSDN.MICROSOFT.COM/EN-US/LIBRARY/MS191475(V=SQL.105).ASPX) and makes it less I/O-efficient at reading contiguous pages on disk. However, this only really affects large range scans from disk. Even for very fragmented indexes, if you are not scanning the table, rebuilding or reorganizing indexes might not help performance. Reduced page density (many gaps causes by page splits and deletes) will cause pages to take up more space on disk and in memory, and require the I/O bandwidth to transfer the data. Again, though, this form of fragmentation won't really affect infrequently modified indexes and so rebuilding them won't help.

Before scheduling index maintenance, ask yourself what performance metrics benefited from the maintenance? Did it reduce I/O significantly? How much did it improve the performance of your most expensive queries? Was the positive impact a sustained one? If the answers to these are "no" or "don't know," then it's probable that regular index maintenance is not the right long-term answer. Finally, it's also worth noting that maintaining small indexes is generally not worthwhile. The commonly cited threshold is around 1,000 pages. Paul Randal suggested these values as guidelines when he was managing the storage engine development team at Microsoft, and they are documented in Books Online. Note, though, that this is *guideline* advice only and may not be appropriate for all environments, as discussed by Paul in his blog post, *Where do the Books Online index fragmentation thresholds come from?* (HTTP://WWW.SQLSKILLS.COM/BLOGS/PAUL/POST/WHERE-DO-THE-BOOKS-ONLINE-INDEX-FRAGMENTATION-THRESHOLDS-COME-FROM.ASPX).

Investigating heavy log-writing transactions

The sys.dm_tran_database_transactions DMV provides useful insight into effects of transaction activity on the transaction log. In their book, *Performance Tuning with SQL Server Dynamic Management Views* (HTTP://WWW.SIMPLE-TALK.COM/BOOKS/SQL-BOOKS/PERFORMANCE-TUNING-WITH-SQL-SERVER-DYNAMIC-MANAGEMENT-VIEWS/), reproduced here with their kind permission, the authors, Louis Davidson and Tim Ford, demonstrate how to use this DMV, and a few others, to investigate transactions that may be causing explosive transaction log growth.

The example in Listing 7.1 reuses the FullRecovery database and PrimaryTable_Large table, from Chapter 6. While not repeated here, we provide the code to re-create this database and table in the code download file. Within an explicit transaction, it rebuilds the clustered index and then investigates log growth.

```
USE FullRecovery
GO
BEGIN TRANSACTION

ALTER INDEX ALL ON dbo.PrimaryTable_Large REBUILD

SELECT DTST.[session_id],
 DES.[login_name] AS [Login Name],
 DB_NAME (DTDT.database_id) AS [Database],
 DTDT.[database_transaction_begin_time] AS [Begin Time],
 DATEDIFF(ms, DTDT.[database_transaction_begin_time], GETDATE())
                                          AS [Duration ms] ,


 CASE DTAT.transaction_type
   WHEN 1 THEN 'Read/write'
    WHEN 2 THEN 'Read-only'
    WHEN 3 THEN 'System'
    WHEN 4 THEN 'Distributed'
  END AS [Transaction Type],
  CASE DTAT.transaction_state
    WHEN 0 THEN 'Not fully initialized'
    WHEN 1 THEN 'Initialized, not started'
    WHEN 2 THEN 'Active'
    WHEN 3 THEN 'Ended'
    WHEN 4 THEN 'Commit initiated'
    WHEN 5 THEN 'Prepared, awaiting resolution'
    WHEN 6 THEN 'Committed'
    WHEN 7 THEN 'Rolling back'
    WHEN 8 THEN 'Rolled back'
  END AS [Transaction State],
WHERE    DB_NAME(DTDT.database_id) = 'FullRecovery'
ORDER BY DTDT.[database_transaction_log_bytes_used] DESC;
-- ORDER BY [Duration ms] DESC;
COMMIT TRANSACTION
DTDT.[database_transaction_log_record_count] AS [Log Records],
 DTDT.[database_transaction_log_bytes_used] AS [Log Bytes Used],
 DTDT.[database_transaction_log_bytes_reserved] AS [Log Bytes RSVPd],
 DEST.[text] AS [Last Transaction Text],
 DEQP.[query_plan] AS [Last Query Plan]
```

```
FROM sys.dm_tran_database_transactions DTDT
INNER JOIN sys.dm_tran_session_transactions DTST
  ON DTST.[transaction_id] = DTDT.[transaction_id]
INNER JOIN sys.[dm_tran_active_transactions] DTAT
  ON DTST.[transaction_id] = DTAT.[transaction_id]
INNER JOIN sys.[dm_exec_sessions] DES
  ON DES.[session_id] = DTST.[session_id]
INNER JOIN sys.dm_exec_connections DEC
  ON DEC.[session_id] = DTST.[session_id]
LEFT JOIN sys.dm_exec_requests DER
  ON DER.[session_id] = DTST.[session_id]
CROSS APPLY sys.dm_exec_sql_text (DEC.[most_recent_sql_handle]) AS DEST
OUTER APPLY sys.dm_exec_query_plan (DER.[plan_handle]) AS DEQP
```

Listing 7.1:   Investigating heavy log-writing transactions.

Figure 7.1 shows some sample output (we split the result set in two, for readability).

	session_id	Database	Begin Time	Duration ms	Transaction Type	Transaction State	Log Records	Log Bytes Used
1	51	FullRecovery	2012-09-17 14:47:38.017	7360	Read/write	Active	20131	166376788

Log Bytes RSVPd	Last Transaction Text		Last Query Plan
958179	BEGIN TRANSACTION	ALTER INDEX ALL ON dbo.Pri...	<ShowPlanXML xmlns="http://schemas.microsoft.com...

Figure 7.1:   Log activities resulting from an index rebuild.

Incidentally, if we rerun this example but with ALTER INDEX...REORGANIZE, then the value in the **Log Bytes Used** column reduces from about 159 MB to around 0.5 MB.

129

Lack of log space reuse

If you suspect that lack of log space reuse is the cause of log growth, your first job is to find out what's preventing reuse. Start by querying `sys.databases`, as shown in Listing 7.2, and see what the value of the column `log_reuse_wait_desc` is for the database mentioned in the error message.

```
SELECT  name ,
        recovery_model_desc ,
        log_reuse_wait_desc
FROM    sys.databases
WHERE   name = 'FullRecovery'
```

Listing 7.2: Examining the value of the `log_reuse_wait_desc` column.

The value of the `log_reuse_wait_desc` column will show the current reason why log space cannot be reused. If you've run the previous example (Listing 7.1), then it's likely that the `FullRecovery` database will display the value `LOG_BACKUP` in this column (more on this in the next section).

It may be that more than one thing is preventing log reuse. The `sys.databases` view will only show one of the reasons. It is therefore possible to resolve one problem, query `sys.databases` again and see a different `log_reuse_wait` reason.

The possible values for `log_reuse_wait_desc` are listed in Books Online (HTTP://MSDN.MICROSOFT.COM/EN-US/LIBRARY/MS178534.ASPX), but we'll cover the most common causes here, and explain how to safely ensure that space can start to get reused.

FULL recovery model without log backups

If the value returned for log_reuse_wait_desc, from the previous sys.databases query, is LOG_BACKUP, then you are suffering from probably the most common cause of a full or large transaction log, namely operating a database in the FULL recovery model (or less common, the BULK_LOGGED recovery model), without taking transaction log backups.

In many editions of SQL Server, the model database is in FULL recovery model by default. Since the model database is a "template" for creating all new SQL Server user databases, the new database inherits this configuration from model.

Using the FULL recovery model is a recommended practice for most production databases, since it allows for point-in-time recovery of the database, minimizing data loss in the event of a disaster. However, a common mistake is then to adopt a backup strategy consisting entirely of full (and possibly differential) database backups without taking frequent transaction log backups. There are two big problems with this strategy:

1. **Taking full database backups only protects the contents of the data file, not the log file.**
   The only way to fully protect the data that has changed since the last full or differential backup, which will be required for point-in-time restores, is to perform a log backup.

2. **Full database backups do not truncate the transaction log.**
   Only a log backup will cause the log file to be truncated. Without the latter, space in the log file is never marked for reuse, and the log file will constantly grow in size.

In order to perform a point-in-time recovery *and* control the size of the log, we must take transaction log backups in conjunction with full database backups or full and differential database backups. For our FullRecovery database, we can take a log backup, as shown in Listing 7.3, and then re-query sys.databases.

```
USE master
GO
BACKUP LOG FullRecovery
TO DISK = 'D:\SQLBackups\FullRecovery_log.trn'
WITH INIT
GO

SELECT   name ,
         recovery_model_desc ,
         log_reuse_wait_desc
FROM     sys.databases
WHERE    name = 'FullRecovery'
```

	name	recovery_model_desc	log_reuse_wait_desc
1	FullRecovery	FULL	NOTHING

Listing 7.3:   Solving the log backup issue.

If a lack of log backups is the cause of log growth problems, the first thing to do is to verify that the database in question really does need to be operating in FULL recovery. This will be true if it must be possible to restore the database to an arbitrary point in time, or to point of failure in the case of a disaster, or if FULL recovery model is required for another reason (such as database mirroring). If the Recovery Point Objective (RPO) in the SLA stipulates a maximum of 15 minutes potential data loss, then it's highly unlikely you can fulfill this with only full and differential database backups and, again, log backups will be necessary.

However, if it turns out there are no log backups simply because they are not required, then the database should not be operating in FULL recovery; we can switch to using the SIMPLE recovery model, where the inactive portion of the transaction log is automatically marked as reusable, at checkpoint.

If the database does need to operate in the FULL recovery model, then start taking log backups, or investigate the need to take more frequent log backups. The frequency of the transaction log backups depends on a number of factors such as the frequency of data changes, and on SLAs for acceptable data loss in the event of a crash. In addition, you should take steps to ensure that the log growth is controlled and predictable in future, as described in the *Proper Log Management* section, later in this chapter.

Active transactions

If the value returned for `log_reuse_wait_desc` is `ACTIVE_TRANSACTION`, then you are suffering from the second most common cause of a full or large transaction log in SQL Server: long-running or uncommitted transactions. Rerun the transaction from Listing 7.1, but without committing it, and then rerun Listing 7.2 and you should see this value listed (don't forget to go back and commit the transaction).

As discussed in the *Log Truncation and Space Reuse* section of Chapter 2, a VLF inside the transaction log can only be truncated when it contains no part of the active log. If the database is using the `FULL` or `BULK_LOGGED` recovery models, only a log backup operation can perform this truncation. Long-running transactions in a database delay truncation of the VLFs that contain the log records generated after the start of the transaction, including the log records generated by changes to data in the database by other concurrent sessions, even when those changes have been committed. Additionally, the amount of space required by a long-running transaction will be increased by space reservations for "compensation log records," which are the log records that would be generated if the transaction were rolled back in the system. This reservation is required to ensure that the transaction can be reverted successfully without running out of log space during the rollback.

Another common cause of the `Active Transaction` value for `log_reuse_wait_desc` is the presence of "orphaned" explicit transactions that somehow never got committed. Applications that allow for user input inside a transaction are especially prone to this kind of problem.

Long-running transactions

One of the most common operations that results in a long-running transaction, which also generates large numbers of log records in a database, is archiving or purging of data from a database. Data retention tends to be an afterthought in database design, usually considered after the database has been active for a period and is approaching the capacity limits of the available storage on a server.

Usually, when the need to archive data arises, the first reaction is to remove the unneeded data from the database using a single DELETE statement, as shown in Listing 7.4. To produce some simple test data, this script uses a simplified version of Jeff Moden's random data generator (see Chapter 1, Listing 1.3), modified slightly to produce dates into 2012.

```
USE FullRecovery ;
GO
IF OBJECT_ID('dbo.LogTest', 'U') IS NOT NULL
    DROP TABLE dbo.LogTest ;
SELECT TOP 500000
        SomeDate = CAST(RAND(CHECKSUM(NEWID())) * 3653.0 + 37534.0 AS DATETIME)
INTO    dbo.LogTest
FROM    sys.all_columns ac1
        CROSS JOIN sys.all_columns ac2 ;

-- delete all but the last 60 days of data
DELETE  dbo.LogTest
WHERE   SomeDate < GETDATE() - 60
```

Listing 7.4: Bulk data deletion.

Depending on the number of rows that exist in the date range to be deleted, this can become a long-running transaction that will cause transaction log growth issues, even when the database is using the SIMPLE recovery model. The presence of cascading FOREIGN KEY constraints or auditing triggers exacerbates the problem. If other tables reference the target table, via FOREIGN KEY constraints designed to CASCADE ON DELETE, then SQL Server will also log details of the rows deleted through the cascading constraint. If the table has a DELETE trigger on it, for auditing data changes, SQL Server will also log the operations performed during the trigger's execution.

To minimize the impact on the transaction log, the data purge operation should be broken down into a number of shorter, individual transactions. There are a number of ways to break a long-running transaction down into smaller batches. If cascading constraints or a DELETE trigger exist for a table, we can perform the DELETE operation inside of a loop, to delete one day of data at a time, as shown in Listing 7.5. Note that, in this simple example, there are insufficient rows in our table to justify use of this technique over a simple DELETE; it is better suited to data purges of millions of rows. Note also that speed is not necessarily the primary concern with batch deletes (Listing 7.5 will run much slower than Listing 7.4). The bigger concerns are avoiding explosive log growth and lock escalation.

```
DECLARE @StopDate DATETIME ,
    @PurgeDate DATETIME
SELECT  @PurgeDate = DATEADD(DAY, DATEDIFF(DAY, 0, MIN(SomeDate)), 0) ,
        @StopDate = DATEADD(DAY, DATEDIFF(DAY, 0, GETDATE()) - 60, 0)
FROM    dbo.LogTest

WHILE @PurgeDate < @StopDate
    BEGIN
        DELETE  dbo.LogTest
        WHERE   SomeDate < @PurgeDate
        SELECT  @PurgeDate = DATEADD(DAY, 1, @PurgeDate)
    END
```

Listing 7.5:   Breaking down data purges into smaller transactions.

Using this model for purging data, the duration of each DELETE transaction is only the time required to delete a single day's data from the table, plus the time required for any triggers or cascading constraints to perform their operations. If the database uses the SIMPLE recovery model, the next checkpoint will truncate the log records generated by each daily purge. If the database uses the FULL or BULK_LOGGED recovery model, the next log backup will truncate the log records generated by each daily purge, as long as no part of the active log exists inside the VLFs containing log records relating to the data purge.

When cascading constraints or auditing triggers are not a factor in the process, we can use a different method to purge the data from the table while minimizing the transaction duration. Instead of performing a single-day DELETE operation, which can affect more or less data, depending on the number of rows that exist for a specific date, use of the TOP operator inside the DELETE statement will limit the number of rows affected by each loop of the operation. By capturing into a variable the number of rows affected by the DELETE operation, using @@ROWCOUNT, the operation can continue to purge data from the table in small batches, until the value of @@ROWCOUNT is less than the number of rows specified in the TOP clause of the DELETE statement, as shown in Listing 7.6.

This method only works when triggers and cascading constraints aren't being used because, when they are, the result of @@ROWCOUNT will not be the actual rows deleted from the base table, but instead the number of rows that are affected by the trigger execution or through enforcing the cascading constraint.

```
DECLARE @Criteria DATETIME ,
    @RowCount INT
SELECT  @Criteria = GETDATE() - 60 ,
        @RowCount = 10000
WHILE @RowCount = 10000
    BEGIN
        DELETE TOP ( 10000 )
        FROM    dbo.LogTest
        WHERE   SomeDate < @Criteria
        SELECT  @RowCount = @@ROWCOUNT
    END
```

Listing 7.6: Using the TOP operator inside the DELETE statement for data purges.

These methods work in any edition of SQL Server 2000, 2005, and 2008 to minimize transaction duration during data purge operations.

However, if the database is SQL Server 2005 or 2008 **Enterprise Edition**, and the data purging process runs regularly, then an even better way to purge the data is to partition the table using a sliding window partition on the column used to delete the data. This will have even less impact on the transaction log, since the partition containing the data can be switched out of the table and truncated, which is an operation for which SQL Server logs only the extent de-allocations.

Managing archiving

It is well outside the scope of this book to delve into full, automated archiving schemes. However, a possible archiving process could involve partitioning, and duplicate schemas between tables, allowing a partition to be switched out of one table and into another one, minimizing the active portion of data in the main OLTP table, but reducing the archiving process to being metadata changes only. Kimberley Tripp has produced a detailed white paper called Partitioned Tables and Indexes in SQL Server 2005, which also covers the sliding window technique, (see HTTP://MSDN.MICROSOFT.COM/EN-US/LIBRARY/ MS345146(V=SQL.90).ASPX).

Uncommitted transactions

By default, SQL Server wraps any data modification statement in an implicit transaction to ensure that, in the event of a failure, SQL Server can roll back the changes already made at the point of failure, returning the data to a consistent state. If the changes succeed, the implicit transaction is committed to the database. In contrast to implicit transactions, which occur automatically, we create explicit transactions in code to wrap multiple changes into a single transaction, ensuring that all the changes can be undone by issuing a ROLLBACK command, or persisted by issuing a COMMIT for the transaction.

When used properly, explicit transactions can ensure that data modifications that span multiple tables complete successfully as a unit, or not at all. When used incorrectly, however, orphaned transactions remain active in the database, preventing truncation of the transaction log, and so resulting in the transaction log growing or filling up.

There are a number of causes of orphaned transactions in SQL Server, and it's beyond the scope of this chapter to investigate them in full detail. However, some of the most common causes are:

- application timeouts caused by a long-running transaction

- incorrect error handling in T-SQL or application code

- failure during trigger execution

- linked server failures resulting in orphaned distributed transactions

- no corresponding COMMIT/ROLLBACK statement to a BEGIN TRANSACTION command.

Once a transaction starts, it will remain active until the connection that created the transaction issues a COMMIT or ROLLBACK statement, or the connection disconnects from the SQL Server (the exception is when using bound connections, which allow sessions to share locks).

Modern applications generally utilize connection pooling, keeping connections to the SQL Server in a pool for reuse by the application, even when the application code calls the Close() method on the connection. It is critical that you understand this last point when troubleshooting orphaned transactions since, even though the connection is reset before being added or returned to the application's connection pool, open transactions continue to exist in the database if they have not been properly terminated.

Identifying the active transaction

The transaction-related Dynamic Management Views (HTTP://MSDN.MICROSOFT.COM/ EN-US/LIBRARY/MS178621.ASPX) provide a wealth of extra information regarding the state of current transactions and the work they perform (see Listing 7.1). However, some DBAs still regard DBCC OPENTRAN as the fastest way to identify whether an orphaned (or just long-running) transaction is the root cause of transaction log growth.

This command can accept the database name as an input parameter in the format DBCC OPENTRAN(DatabaseName) where DatabaseName is the name of the database to check for open transactions. If an active transaction exists in the database, this command will output information similar to that shown in Listing 7.7.

```
DBCC OPENTRAN (FullRecovery)

Transaction information for database 'FullRecovery'.

Oldest active transaction:
    SPID (server process ID): 56
    UID (user ID) : -1
    Name            : user_transaction
    LSN             : (897:15322:1)
    Start time      : Sep 18 2012  1:01:29:390PM
    SID             : 0x010500000000000515000000fd43461e19525f12828ba628ee0a0000
DBCC execution completed. If DBCC printed error messages, contact your system
administrator.
```

Listing 7.7:   Sample output from DBCC OPENTRAN.

DBCC OPENTRAN reports only the oldest active transaction, and the primary indicator of whether or not the active transaction is problematic is the Start Time. Generally, uncommitted transactions that become problematic with regard to transaction log growth have been open for a long period of time.

The other important piece of information is the SPID (server process ID; in the DMVs this is replaced by session_id), which identifies the session that created the open transaction. We can use the SPID to determine whether the transaction is actually an orphaned transaction or just a long-running one, by querying the sysprocesses view (in SQL Server 2000) or the sys.dm_exec_sessions and sys.dm_exec_connections DMVs in SQL Server 2005 and later, as shown in Listing 7.8.

Note that the `sysprocesses` view is still available in SQL Server 2005 and later for backwards compatibility. In each query, simply replace the `session_id` value with the one you saw when running Listing 7.7 (we have commented out certain columns, simply for readability of the output).

```
USE master
GO
SELECT  spid ,
        status ,
--      hostname ,
--      program_name ,
--      loginame ,
        login_time ,
        last_batch ,
        ( SELECT    text
          FROM      ::
                    fn_get_sql(sql_handle)
        ) AS [sql_text]
FROM    sysprocesses
WHERE   spid = 56

USE FullRecovery
GO
SELECT  s.session_id ,
        s.status ,
--      s.host_name ,
--      s.program_name ,
--      s.login_name ,
        s.login_time ,
        s.last_request_start_time ,
        s.last_request_end_time ,
        t.text

FROM    sys.dm_exec_sessions s
        JOIN sys.dm_exec_connections c ON s.session_id = c.session_id
        CROSS APPLY sys.dm_exec_sql_text(c.most_recent_sql_handle) t
WHERE   s.session_id = 56
```

	spid	status	login_time	last_batch	sql_text
1	56	sleeping	2012-09-18 11:41:08.510	2012-09-18 13:01:30.323	BEGIN TRAN DELETE dbo.LogTest WHERE SomeDa...

	session_id	status	login_time	last_request_start_time	last_request_end_time	text
1	56	sleeping	2012-09-18 11:41:08.510	2012-09-18 13:01:27.670	2012-09-18 13:01:30.323	BEGIN TRAN DELETE dbo.LogTest WHERE SomeDa...

Listing 7.8: Identifying orphaned or long-running transactions using the DMVs.

If the session is in a runnable, running, or suspended status, then it is likely that the source of the problem is a long-running, rather than orphaned, transaction. However, only further investigation will confirm. It is possible that an earlier transaction failed and the connection was reset, for use under connection pooling, and that the currently executing statement is not associated with the open transaction.

In SQL Server 2005 and later, we can use the `sys.dm_tran_session_transactions` and `sys.dm_tran_database_transactions` DMVs to gather information specific to the open transaction, including the transaction start time, number of log records used by the open transaction, as well as the bytes of log space used, as we saw previously in Listing 7.1. Listing 7.9 shows a simplified version, with sample output.

```
SELECT   st.session_id ,
         st.is_user_transaction ,
         dt.database_transaction_begin_time ,
         dt.database_transaction_log_record_count ,
         dt.database_transaction_log_bytes_used
FROM     sys.dm_tran_session_transactions st
         JOIN sys.dm_tran_database_transactions dt
                   ON st.transaction_id = dt.transaction_id
                      AND dt.database_id = DB_ID('FullRecovery')
WHERE st.session_id = 56
```

	session_id	is_user_transaction	database_transaction_begin_time	database_transaction_log_record_count	database_transaction_log_bytes_used
1	56	1	2012-09-18 13:01:29.390	489153	48915332

Listing 7.9: Gathering information about the open transaction.

Unless the application was specifically designed to check for, and handle, orphaned transactions, the only way to clear the transaction is to KILL the session, which will cause the transaction to roll back as the connection terminates, allowing the space in the log to be made available for reuse during the next log backup. However, the ramifications of performing the rollback must be understood.

Other possible causes of log growth

In addition to those previously identified, there are a few other problems that may prevent reuse of space in the log, and so lead to excessive log growth. I'll cover a few of them here, but for further discussion on these issues, please see Gail Shaw's article, *Why is my transaction log full?* at HTTP://WWW.SQLSERVERCENTRAL.COM/ARTICLES/ TRANSACTION+LOG/72488/.

Replication

During transactional replication, it is the job of the log reader agent to read the transaction log, looking for log records that are associated with changes that need to be replicated to subscribers (i.e. are "pending replication"). Once the changes are replicated, it marks the log entry as "replicated." Slow or delayed log reader activity can lead to records being left as "pending replication" for long periods, during which time they will remain part of the active log, and so the parent VLF cannot be truncated. A similar problem exists for log records required by the Change Data Capture (CDC) feature.

In either case, the log_reuse_wait_desc column of sys.databases will show REPLICATION as the root cause of the problem. The problem will also reveal itself in the form of bottlenecks in the throughput performance of the transaction log disk array, specifically, delayed read operations under concurrent write loads. Writes to the log file occur sequentially, but read operations associated with the log reader agent and log backups read the file sequentially as well. Having sequential reads and writes occurring at the same time can, depending on the level of activity in the system and the size of the active portion of the log, result in random I/O activity as the disk heads have to change position to read from the beginning of the active log and then write to the end of the active log. We can use the disk latency Perfmon counters, `Physical Disk\Disk Reads/sec` and `Physical Disk\Disk Writes/sec` counters to troubleshoot this type of problem. See Chapter 2 of the free eBook, *Troubleshooting SQL Server* (HTTP://WWW. SIMPLE-TALK.COM/BOOKS/SQL-BOOKS/TROUBLESHOOTING-SQL-SERVER-A-GUIDE-FOR-THE-ACCIDENTAL-DBA/) for further details on this topic.

The first step in troubleshooting these `REPLICATION` wait issues is to verify that the log reader SQL Agent jobs are actually running. If they are not, attempt to start them. If this fails, you'll need to find out why.

If the jobs are running but the `REPLICATION` waits persist, and the transaction log is growing rapidly, you need to find some way to get the relevant log entries marked as "replicated" so that space in their parent VLFs can be reused. Unfortunately, there is no perfect solution that will avoid side effects to replication or CDC in the environment, but you could try one of the solutions below.

- **In the case of transactional replication, use the `sp_repldone` command** to mark all of the log records currently waiting on the log reader as replicated, but this will require re-initialization of the subscribers. With CDC, this command will not resolve the problem with transaction log growth.

- **Disabling CDC or replication and performing a manual resynchronization of the data**. Having disabled CDC or replication, the pending replication log records in the transaction log will no longer be pending and the next log backup, in `FULL` or `BULK_LOGGED` recovery, or `CHECKPOINT` operation in `SIMPLE` recovery, will clear them out. However, the trade-off is that the environment will require manual synchronization of the data for CDC, or it will require re-initialization of the subscribers for replication, if these features are added back to the database.

Remember that simply switching to the **SIMPLE** recovery model, in the hope of truncating the log, will not work since replication and CDC are both supported using **SIMPLE** recovery, and the log records will continue to be required until the log reader SQL Agent process processes them.

Snapshot Replication schema change issue

There is a known issue with Snapshot Replication in SQL Server 2005 that causes log entries that are marked for replication of schema changes not to be unmarked when the changes are replicated. This problem is explained in the following blog post that also explains how to work around the issue by using `sp_repldone`: *Size of the transaction log increasing and cannot be truncated or shrunk due to Snapshot Replication* (HTTP://BLOGS.MSDN.COM/B/SQLSERVERFAQ/ARCHIVE/2009/06/01/SIZE-OF-THE-TRANSACTION-LOG-INCREASING-AND-CANNOT-BE-TRUNCATED-OR-SHRINKED-DUE-TO-SNAPSHOT-REPLICATION.ASPX).

ACTIVE_BACKUP_OR_RESTORE

When the `log_reuse_wait_desc` column shows `ACTIVE_BACKUP_OR_RESTORE` as the current wait description, a long-running full or differential backup of the database is the most likely cause of the log reuse problems. During a full or differential backup of the database, the backup process delays log truncation so that the active portion of the transaction log can be included as a part of the full backup. This allows changes made to database pages during the backup operation to be undone when the backup is restored **WITH RECOVERY**, to bring the database to a consistent state. If such waits are causing persistent problems, you'll need to investigate ways to optimize the backup process, such as by improving the performance of the backups (via backup compression) or improving the performance of the underlying disk I/O system.

DATABASE_MIRRORING

When the `log_reuse_wait_desc` column shows `DATABASE_MIRRORING`, as the current wait description, asynchronous database mirroring operations may be the cause of the log reuse issues.

In synchronous mirroring, transactions on the principal are only committed once their related log records have been transferred to the mirror database. For asynchronous database mirroring, the log records are transferred later and the principal's log can't be truncated until they are. When mirroring problems arise, a large number of log records on the principal can remain part of the active log, preventing log space reuse, until copied over to the mirror.

For synchronous database mirroring, we may see a value of `DATABASE_MIRRORING` if the mirror is not contactable, due to a broken or very slow connection, or suspension of the mirroring session. For asynchronous database mirroring, we may well see this value during normal operation, as well as during connection problems.

In such cases, I would first check the status of the mirroring session for the affected database(s). If they are not synchronizing correctly, then you will need to troubleshoot the cause of the failed connection between the principal and the mirror. One of the most common problems with database mirroring, when certificates are used to secure the endpoints, is the expiration of the certificates, requiring that they be re-created. A full discussion of troubleshooting mirroring connectivity problems is outside the scope of this book but, unless the databases are properly synchronizing so that the log records are being sent to the mirror, the active portion of the transaction log on the principal will continue to grow and not be able to be truncated without breaking the mirroring setup.

If the transaction rate on the principal greatly exceeds the rate at which log records can be transferred to the mirror, then the log on the principal can grow rapidly. If the mirror server is being used for reporting, by creating snapshots, verify that the disk I/O configuration for the mirror is not saturated, by using the disk latency Perfmon counters mentioned earlier. If this is where the problem is, eliminating use of the mirror server for reporting may provide temporary relief of the problem. If the problem is strictly the sheer volume of transactions and the database is not running on SQL Server 2008 or higher, then upgrading may be able to resolve the problem due to the use of log stream compression in SQL Server 2008 and beyond.

The best approach is to determine the cause of the mirroring issue and resolve it. For example, tuning operations that produce a significant number of log records, such as bulk loading data, or reorganizing indexes, may reduce the impact to the system overall during the operation.

Handling a Transaction Log Full Error

In the worst case, transaction log mismanagement or sudden, rapid, log growth can cause a transaction log to grow and eventually devour all available space on its drive. At this point it can grow no more, you'll encounter Error 9002, the **transaction log full** error, and the database will become read-only.

Despite the urgency of this problem, it's important to react calmly, and avoid the sort of "spontaneous" solutions that are covered in the following section, *Mismanagement or What Not To Do*. Obviously the pressing concern is to allow SQL Server to continue to write to the log, by making more space available. The first port of call is to establish if the cause is a lack of log backups. Run the query in Listing 7.1 and if the value for the log_reuse_wait_desc column is Log Backup then this is the likely cause of the issue. A query to the backupset table (HTTP://MSDN.MICROSOFT.COM/EN-US/LIBRARY/MS186299. ASPX) in the MSDB database, as shown in Listing 7.10, will confirm whether or not log backups are being taken on the database, and when the last one was taken.

```
USE msdb ;
SELECT    backup_set_id ,
          backup_start_date ,
          backup_finish_date ,
          backup_size ,
          recovery_model ,
          [type]
FROM      dbo.backupset
WHERE     database_name = 'DatabaseName'
```

Listing 7.10: Which backups were taken, and when.

In the `type` column, a `D` represents a database backup, `L` represents a log backup and `I` represents a differential backup. If there are no log backups, or they are very infrequent, then your best course of action is to take a log backup (assuming the database is operating in `FULL` or `BULK_LOGGED` recovery model). Hopefully, this will free up substantial space within the log and you can then implement an appropriate log backup scheme, and log file growth management strategy.

If, for some reason, it is not possible to perform a log backup due to a lack of disk space, or the time it would take to perform a log backup exceeds the acceptable time to resolve the problem, then, depending on the disaster recovery policy for the database in question, it might be acceptable to force a truncation of the log by temporarily switching the database to the `SIMPLE` recovery model in order that inactive VLFs in the log can be truncated on `CHECKPOINT`. You can then switch the recovery model back to `FULL` and perform a new full database backup (or a differential backup, assuming a full backup was taken at some previous time) to restart the log chain for point-in-time recovery. Of course, you'll still need to investigate the problem fully, in order to make sure that the space isn't simply devoured again. Bear in mind also that, as discussed previously, if the problem preventing space reuse is anything other than `Log Backup`, then this technique won't work, since those records will simply remain part of the active log, preventing truncation.

If a lack of log backups isn't the problem, or taking a log backup doesn't solve the problem, then investigating the cause will require a little more time. If it is quick and easy to make extra space on the log drive then do so. This might mean shifting off other files, or adding capacity to the current log drive, or adding an extra log file on a different disk array, but it will buy you the bit of breathing space you need to get the database out of read-only mode, and perform a log backup.

If a log backup fails to free up space, you need to find out what is preventing space reuse in the log. Interrogate sys.databases (Listing 7.1) to find out if anything is preventing reuse of space in the log, and take appropriate action, as described in the earlier *Lack of log space reuse* section.

If this reveals nothing, you'll need to investigate further and find out which operations are causing the excessive logging that led to the log growth, as described in the *Diagnosing a Runaway Transaction Log* section.

Ultimately, having resolved any space reuse issue, we may still have a log file that is consuming the vast majority of the space on the drive. As a one-off measure, i.e. assuming we will take steps to ensure proper management of log growth in the future (see the *Proper Log Management* section, following shortly), it is acceptable to use DBCC SHRINKFILE (see HTTP://MSDN.MICROSOFT.COM/EN-US/LIBRARY/MS189493.ASPX) to reclaim the space used by a bloated transaction log file. We'll provide an example of how to do this in Chapter 8.

We can either specify a target_size to which to shrink the log file, or we can specify 0 (zero) as the target size and shrink the log to its smallest possible size, and then immediately resize it to a sensible size using ALTER DATABASE. The latter is the recommended way, as it minimizes fragmentation of the log file. This fragmentation issue is the main reason why you should *never* schedule regular DBCC SHRINKFILE tasks as a means of controlling the size of the log; we discuss this in more detail in the next section.

Mismanagement or What Not To Do

Unfortunately, a quick search of the Internet for "Transaction Log Full" will return a number of forum threads, blog posts, and even articles published on seemingly reputable SQL Server sites, which recommend remedial action that is, frankly, dangerous. We'll cover a few of the more popular suggestions here.

Detach database, delete log file

The idea here is that you clear all users off the database, detach the database (or shut it down), delete the log file (or rename it) and then re-attach the database, causing a new log file to be created at whatever size is dictated by the `model` database. This is arguably the most appalling of all the terrible ways to handle a full transaction log. It can result in the database failing to start, leaving it in the `RECOVERY_PENDING` state.

Depending on whether or not the database had been cleanly shut down at the time of the log deletion, the database may not be able to perform the `UNDO` and `REDO` operations that are a normal part of the database recovery process, because the transaction log is missing, and so can't return the database to a consistent state. When the log file is missing, and the database requires the transaction log to perform crash recovery, the database will fail to start up properly and the only recourse will be to restore the database from the most recent backup available, which will most likely result in data loss.

Creating, detaching, re-attaching, and fixing a suspect database

Under specific circumstances, it may be possible to hack the existing database into a configuration that allows the transaction log to be rebuilt, although it may compromise the integrity of the data contained in the database. This type of operation is, at best, a last-ditch effort that may be used when there is absolutely no other way of recovering the database data, and it is not a recommended practice of the authors, technical editors, or anyone else involved in the authoring of this book. For an explanation of how to attempt hacking a database back into SQL Server where the transaction log file has been deleted, see Paul Randal's blog post, Creating, detaching, re-attaching, and fixing a suspect database (HTTP:// WWW.SQLSKILLS.COM/BLOGS/PAUL/POST/TECHED-DEMO-CREATING-DETACHING-RE-ATTACHING-AND- FIXING-A-SUSPECT-DATABASE.ASPX).

Forcing log file truncation

In SQL Server 2000 and 2005, `BACKUP LOG WITH TRUNCATE_ONLY` was a supported (though deprecated in SQL 2005) way of forcing SQL Server to truncate the transaction log, while the database was operating in the `FULL` or `BULK_LOGGED` model. Using this command does not actually make a backup copy of the contents of the log; the records in the truncated VLFs are discarded. So, unlike with a normal log backup, you're destroying your LSN chain and you will only be able to restore to a point in time in any previous log backup files. Also, even though the database is set to `FULL` (or `BULK_LOGGED`) recovery, it will actually, from that point on, operate in an auto-truncate mode, continuing to truncate inactive VLFs on checkpoint. In order to get the database operating in `FULL` recovery again, and restart the LSN chain, you'd need to perform a full (or differential) backup.

This command was often used without people realizing the implications it had for disaster recovery, and it was deprecated in SQL Server 2005 and removed from SQL Server 2008. Unfortunately, an even more insidious variation of this technique, which continues to be supported, has crept up to take its place, and that is `BACKUP LOG TO DISK='NUL'`, where `NUL` is a "virtual file" that discards any data that is written to it. The really nasty twist to this technique is that, unlike with `BACKUP LOG WITH TRUNCATE_ONLY`, SQL Server is unaware that the log records have simply been discarded. As far as SQL Server is concerned, a log backup has been performed, the log records are safely stored in a backup file so the LSN chain is intact, and any inactive VLFs in the live log can safely be truncated. Any subsequent, conventional log backups will succeed but will be entirely useless from the point of view of disaster recovery since a log backup file is "missing" and so the database can only be restored to some point in time covered by the last standard log backup that was taken before `BACKUP LOG TO DISK='NUL'` was issued.

Do not use either of these techniques. The right way to "force" log truncation is to temporarily switch the database into the `SIMPLE` recovery model, as discussed earlier.

Scheduled shrinking of the transaction log

As discussed in the *Handling a Transaction Log Full Error* section, in rare circumstances where transaction log growth has occurred due to a lack of management, and where the log growth is currently being actively managed, using `DBCC SHRINKFILE` to reclaim the space used by the transaction log file is an acceptable operation.

However, we should never shrink the transaction log as part of normal, scheduled maintenance operations. The reason for this is that every time we shrink the log, it will need to grow again immediately to store log records for subsequent transactions. As discussed previously in the *Sizing and Growing the Log* section, the transaction log cannot take advantage of instant file initialization, so all log growths incur the cost to zero-byte the storage space that SQL Serve needs to allocate. In addition, if we rely on auto-growth for transaction log growth (see the next section for a fuller discussion), excessive VLFs can accumulate in the log file and this log fragmentation will impact the performance of any process that needs to read the log file and, if fragmentation gets really bad, possibly even the performance of data modifications.

The best practice for the transaction log file continues to be to size it appropriately up front, so it does not have to grow under normal operations. Then, monitor its usage periodically to determine if the need to grow it manually occurs, allowing you to determine the appropriate growth size and determine the number and size of VLFs that will be added to the log file. We'll discuss this in more detail in Chapter 8.

Proper Log Management

In the absence of any unexpected operations or problems that have resulted in unusual log growth (replication problems, uncommitted transactions, and so on, as discussed earlier), if the transaction log associated with a FULL recovery model database fills up, and is forced to grow, there are really only two causes:

- the size of the log file was too small to support the volume of data changes that were occurring in the database
- the frequency of log backups was insufficient to allow rapid reuse of space within the log file.

The best thing to do, if you can't increase the frequency of the log backups by decreasing the amount of time between them, is to manually grow the log file to a size that prevents it from having to grow using auto-growth when under load, and then leave the log file that size. Having a large transaction log file that we've grown manually to minimize the number of VLFs is not a bad thing, even if the log file has free space a majority of the time. There will be more about this in Chapter 8.

Summary

The transaction log is critical to the operation of a SQL Server database, and the ability to minimize data loss in the event of a disaster. In a situation where the log is growing explosively, or is even full, the DBA needs to act very quickly to diagnose and fix the problem, but it's also important to act calmly, and avoid unthinking reactions such as forcing log truncation, then scheduling regular log shrinks, which will cause more harm than good.

Acknowledgements

Many thanks to Jonathan Kehayias, lead author of *Troubleshooting SQL Server* (HTTP://WWW.SIMPLE-TALK.COM/BOOKS/SQL-BOOKS/TROUBLESHOOTING-SQL-SERVER-A-GUIDE-FOR-THE-ACCIDENTAL-DBA/), available as a free eBook, for contributing additional material to this chapter.

Chapter 8: Optimizing Log Throughput

We'll start with a brief review of the ideal storage architecture for the log file, for maximum log throughput, and then take a deeper look at how log fragmentation can affect the performance of operations that need to read the log, such as log backups, or the crash recovery process.

Finally, we'll consider best practices in managing log sizing and growth, and the correct response to explosive log growth and fragmentation.

Physical Architecture

The correct physical hardware and architecture will help ensure that you get the best possible log throughput, and there are a few "golden rules." Others have covered this before, notably Kimberly Tripp in her much referenced blog post, *8 Steps to better Transaction Log throughput*, (HTTP://WWW.SQLSKILLS.COM/BLOGS/KIMBERLY/POST/8-STEPS-TO-BETTER-TRANSACTION-LOG-THROUGHPUT.ASPX), so we won't go into detail again here.

Note that in designing the underlying physical architecture for the log file, our primary goal is to optimize log *write* throughput. SQL Server writes to the log in response to every transaction that adds, removes or modifies data, as well as in response to database maintenance operations such as index rebuilds or reorganization, statistics updates, and more.

You only need one log file

There is no performance gain, in terms of log throughput, from multiple log files. SQL Server does not write log records in parallel to multiple log files. There's one situation when SQL Server will write to all the log files, and that's when it updates the header in each log file. The log header is a mirror of the database header page, and SQL Server writes to it to update various LSNs, such as the last checkpoint, the oldest open transaction, the last log backup, and so on. This sometimes tricks people into thinking that SQL Server is logging to all the log files, when it is only updating the header.

If a database has four log files, SQL Server will write log records to Log File 1, until it is full, then fill Files 2, 3 and 4, and then attempt to wrap back around and start writing to File 1 again. We can see this in action simply by creating a database with several log files (or by adding more files to an existing database). Listing 8.1 creates a **Persons** database, with a primary data file and two log files, each on a separate drive.

Data and backup file locations

All of the examples in this chapter assume that data and log files are located in `'D:\SQLData'` *and all backups in* `'D:\SQLBackups'`, *respectively. When running the examples, simply modify these locations as appropriate for your system (and note that in a real system, we wouldn't store data and log files on the same drive!).*

Note that we've based the **SIZE** and **FILEGROWTH** settings for the data and log files on those for **AdventureWorks2008**. The code for this example (Listings 8.1–8.3) is in the **YouOnlyNeed1Log.sql** file, in the code download.

```
USE master
GO
IF DB_ID('Persons') IS NOT NULL
    DROP DATABASE Persons;
GO

CREATE DATABASE [Persons] ON PRIMARY
  (   NAME = N'Persons'
    , FILENAME = N'D:\SQLData\Persons.mdf'
    , SIZE = 199680KB
    , FILEGROWTH = 16384KB
  )
 LOG ON
  (   NAME = N'Persons_log'
    , FILENAME = N'D:\SQLData\Persons_log.ldf'
    , SIZE = 2048KB
    , FILEGROWTH = 16384KB
  ),
  (   NAME = N'Persons_log2'
    , FILENAME = N'C:\SQLData\Persons_log2.ldf'
    , SIZE = 2048KB
    , FILEGROWTH = 16384KB
  )
GO

ALTER DATABASE Persons SET RECOVERY FULL;

USE master
GO
BACKUP DATABASE Persons
TO DISK ='D:\SQLBackups\Persons_full.bak'
WITH INIT;
GO
```

Listing 8.1: Create the Persons database with two log files.

Next, Listing 8.2 creates a sample Persons table.

```
USE Persons
GO
IF EXISTS ( SELECT  *
            FROM    sys.objects
            WHERE   object_id = OBJECT_ID(N'dbo.Persons')
                    AND type = N'U' )
    DROP TABLE dbo.Persons;
GO

CREATE TABLE dbo.Persons
    (
      PersonID INT NOT NULL
                  IDENTITY ,
      FName VARCHAR(20) NOT NULL ,
      LName VARCHAR(30) NOT NULL ,
      Email VARCHAR(7000) NOT NULL
    );
GO
```

Listing 8.2:   Create the Persons table.

Now, we'll add 15K rows to the table and run DBCC LOGINFO. Note that in our tests, we filled the Persons table with data from the Person.Contact table in the Adventure-Works 2005 database. However, the code download file contains alternative code, which will work with AdventureWorks2008 and AdventureWorks2012.

```
INSERT  INTO dbo.Persons
        ( FName ,
          LName ,
          Email
        )
        SELECT TOP 15000
          LEFT(aw1.FirstName, 20) ,
                LEFT(aw1.LastName, 30) ,
                aw1.EmailAddress
        FROM    AdventureWorks2005.Person.Contact aw1
        CROSS JOIN AdventureWorks2005.Person.Contact aw2;
GO

USE Persons
GO
DBCC LOGINFO;
```

	FileId	FileSize	StartOffset	FSeqNo	Status	Parity	CreateLSN
1	2	458752	8192	36	2	64	0
2	2	458752	466944	37	2	64	0
3	2	458752	925696	38	2	64	0
4	2	712704	1384448	39	2	64	0
5	2	4194304	2097152	0	0	0	39000000097600656
6	2	4194304	6291456	0	0	0	39000000097600656
7	2	4194304	10485760	0	0	0	39000000097600656
8	2	4194304	14680064	0	0	0	39000000097600656
9	3	458752	8192	40	2	64	0
10	3	458752	466944	41	2	64	0
11	3	458752	925696	42	2	64	0
12	3	712704	1384448	0	0	0	0

Listing 8.3: Populate Persons and check the VLFs.

SQL Server is sequentially filling the VLFs in the primary log file (FileID 2), followed by the secondary one (FileID 3). It has also auto-grown the primary log file (please refer back to Chapter 2 for a more detailed example of how SQL Server auto-grows the transaction log).

If we continue to add rows, SQL Server will continue to grow both files as required, and fill the VLFs sequentially, one VLF at a time. Figure 8.1 shows the situation after rerunning Listing 8.3 for 95,000 rows (110K rows added in total). Now we have 12 VLFs for the primary log file and 8 for the secondary log file.

	FileId	FileSize	StartOffset	FSeqNo	Status	Parity	CreateLSN
4	2	712704	1384448	39	2	64	0
5	2	4194304	2097152	44	2	64	39000000097600656
6	2	4194304	6291456	45	2	64	39000000097600656
7	2	4194304	10485760	46	2	64	39000000097600656
8	2	4194304	14680064	47	2	64	39000000097600656
9	2	4194304	18874368	0	0	0	47000000625600655
10	2	4194304	23068672	0	0	0	47000000625600655
11	2	4194304	27262976	0	0	0	47000000625600655
12	2	4194304	31457280	0	0	0	47000000625600655
13	3	458752	8192	40	2	64	0
14	3	458752	466944	41	2	64	0
15	3	458752	925696	42	2	64	0
16	3	712704	1384448	43	2	64	0
17	3	4194304	2097152	48	2	64	45000000649600655
18	3	4194304	6291456	0	0	0	45000000649600655
19	3	4194304	10485760	0	0	0	45000000649600655
20	3	4194304	14680064	0	0	0	45000000649600655

Figure 8.1: Sequential use of two log files.

In this situation, any operation that reads the log will start by reading a block of four VLFs in the primary log (FSeqNo 36–39), followed by four blocks in the secondary log (FSeqNo 40–43), followed four blocks in the primary log, and so on. This is why multiple log files can reduce I/O efficiency, as we'll discuss further in the next section.

The only reason to add an additional log file is in exceptional circumstances where, for example, the disk housing the log file is full (see Chapter 6) and we need, temporarily, to add an additional log file as the quickest means to get the SQL Server out of read-only mode. However, as soon as it's no longer required the additional file should be removed, as discussed later, in the section, *What to Do If Things Go Wrong*.

Use a dedicated drive/array for the log file

There are several reasons why it's a good idea to house the data files on separate disks from the log file. Firstly, this architecture offers better chances of recovery in the event of disk failure. For example, if the array housing the data files suffers catastrophic failure, the log file doesn't go down with the ship. We may still be able to perform a tail log backup, and so recover the database to a point very close the time of failure (see Chapter 5).

Secondly, it's a good idea to separate data file I/O from log file I/O in order to optimize I/O efficiency. SQL Server databases perform both random and sequential I/O operations.

Sequential I/O is any form of I/O where SQL Server can read or write blocks without requiring repositioning of the disk head on the drive. SQL Server uses sequential I/O for read-ahead operations, and for all transaction log operations, and it is the fastest I/O type, using conventional disks.

Random I/O is any operation where reading or writing of blocks requires the disk head to change positions on the platter. This incurs seek latency I/O and reduces both throughput (MB/s) and performance (IOPS) relative to sequential I/O. Read operations in general, especially in OLTP systems, are random I/O operations, reading relatively small blocks of pages sequentially as a part of larger random I/O requests.

By separating mainly random from mainly sequential I/O, we avoid contention between the two, and improve overall I/O efficiency. Furthermore, the optimum configuration for log files is not necessarily the same as for the data files. By separating data and log files, we can configure each I/O subsystem as appropriate for that type of I/O activity, for example by choosing the optimal RAID configuration for the disk array (see the next section).

Finally, note that a single log file on a dedicated drive/array allows the disk head to stay more or less steady as SQL Server writes sequentially to the log. However, with multiple log files on a single drive/array, the disk head will need to jump between each log; we don't have sequential writes without disk seeks, and so we reduce the efficiency of sequential I/O.

Ideally, every database will have one log file on a dedicated disk array, though in many systems this remains an ideal rather than a practical reality.

For similar reasons, relating to sequential I/O efficiency, it's also important to defragment the physical disk drives before we create the log file.

Use RAID 10 for log drives, if possible

RAID, an acronym for Redundant Array of Independent Disks, is the technology used to achieve the following objectives:

- **Increase levels of I/O performance**, measured in Input/Output Operations Per Second (IOPS), which is roughly (`MB/sec / IO size in KB`)*1024.

- **Increase levels of I/O throughput**, measured in Megabytes Per Second (MB/sec) which is roughly (`IOPS*IO size in KB`)/1024.

- **Increase storage capacity available in a single logical device** – you can't purchase a single 5-TB disk yet, but you can have a 5-TB disk in Windows by, for example, using RAID to stripe six 1-TB drives in a RAID 5 array.

- **Gain data redundancy** through storing parity information across multiple disks, or using mirroring of the physical disks in the array.

The choice of RAID level is heavily dependent on the nature of the workload that the disk array must support. For example, as discussed earlier, the difference in the nature of the I/O workloads for data and log files means that different RAID configurations may be applicable in each case.

In terms of I/O throughput and performance, we should strive to optimize the log file array for sequential writes. Most experts acknowledge **RAID 1+0** as the best option in this regard, though it also happens to be the most expensive in terms of cost per GB of storage space.

Deeper into RAID

A full review the pros and cons of each RAID level is out of scope for this book. For further information, we refer you to Chapter 2 of the book, Troubleshooting SQL Server, by Jonathan Kehayias and Ted Krueger (available as a paid-for paperback or free eBook): HTTP://WWW.SIMPLE-TALK.COM/BOOKS/ SQL-BOOKS/TROUBLESHOOTING-SQL-SERVER-A-GUIDE-FOR-THE-ACCIDENTAL-DBA/.

RAID 1+0 is a nested RAID level known as a "striped pair of mirrors." It provides redundancy by first mirroring each disk, using RAID 1, and then striping those mirrored disks with RAID 0, to improve performance. There is a significant monetary cost increase associated with this configuration since only half of the disk space is available for use. However, this configuration offers the best configuration for redundancy since, potentially, it allows for multiple disk failures while still leaving the system operational, and without degrading system performance.

A common and somewhat cheaper alternative is RAID 5, "striping with parity," which stripes data across multiple disks, as per RAID 0, and stores parity data in order to provide protection from single disk failure. RAID 5 requires fewer disks for the same storage capacity, compared to RAID 1+0, and offers excellent read performance. However, the need to maintain parity data incurs a performance penalty for writes. While this is less of a problem for modern storage arrays, it's the reason why many DBAs don't recommend it for the transaction log files, which primarily perform sequential writes and require the lowest possible write latency.

If, as per our previous suggestion, you are able to isolate a single database's log file on a dedicated array, at least for those databases with the heaviest I/O workload, then it may be possible to use the more expensive RAID 1+0 for those arrays, and RAID 5, or RAID 1, for lower workload databases.

To give an idea of the I/O performance offers by various RAID levels, following are three possible RAID configurations for a 400 GB database that performs a balanced mix of random read and write operations, along with the resulting *theoretical* I/O throughput rates, based on a 64K random I/O workload for SQL Server.

1. RAID 1 using 2 x 600 GB 15K RPM disks =>**185** IOPS at **11.5** MB/sec.

2. RAID 5 using 5 x 146 GB 15K RPM disks =>**345** IOPS at **22** MB/sec.

3. RAID 10 using 14 x 73 GB 15K RPM disks => **1609** IOPS at **101** MB/sec.

Remember, though, that these numbers are theoretical, based only on the potential I/O capacity of the disks in a given configuration. They take no account of other factors that can, and will, have an impact on overall throughput, including RAID controller cache size and configuration, RAID stripe size, disk partition alignment, or NTFS format allocation unit sizes. The only way to be sure that your selected disk configuration will cope gracefully with the workload placed on it by your databases is to perform proper benchmarking of the I/O subsystem, prior to usage.

> *Benchmarking storage configurations for SQL Server*
>
> *A number of tools exist for measuring the I/O throughput of a given configuration, the two most common tools being* **SQLIO** (HTTP://WWW.MICROSOFT.COM/DOWNLOAD/EN/DETAILS.ASPX?ID=20163) *and* **IOmeter** (HTTP://WWW.IOMETER.ORG/). *In addition, there is* **SQLIOSim**, *for testing the reliability and integrity of a disk configuration* (HTTP://SUPPORT.MICROSOFT.COM/KB/231619/EN-US).

Log Fragmentation and Operations that Read the Log

As discussed in Chapter 2, internally SQL Server breaks down a transaction log file into a number of sub-files called **virtual log files** (VLFs). SQL Server determines the number and size of VLFs to allocate to a log file, upon creation, and then will add a predetermined number of VLFs each time the log grows, based on the size of the auto-growth increment, as follows (though, for very small growth increments, it will sometimes add fewer than four VLFs):

- <64 MB – each auto-growth event will create 4 new VLFs.

- 64MB to 1 GB = 8 VLFs.

- >1 GB = 16 VLFs.

For example, if we create a 64 MB log file and set it to auto-grow in 16 MB increments, then the log file will initially have 8 VLFs, each 8 MB in size, and SQL Server will add 4 VLFs, each 4 MB in size, every time the log grows. If the database attracts many more users than anticipated, but the file settings are left untouched, by the time the log reaches 10 GB in size, it will have grown about 640 times, and will have over 2,500 VLFs.

Towards the other end of the scale, if we grow a log in 16 GB chunks, then each growth will add 16 VLFs, each 1 GB in size. With large VLFs, we risk tying up large portions of the log that SQL Server cannot truncate, and if some factor further delays truncation, meaning the log has to grow, the growth will be rapid.

The trick is to obtain the right balance. The maximum recommended auto-growth size is about 8 GB (advice offered by Paul Randal in his *Log File Internals and Maintenance* video, HTTP://TECHNET.MICROSOFT.COM/EN-US/SQLSERVER/GG313762.ASPX). Conversely, the growth increments must be large enough to avoid an unreasonably large number of VLFs.

There are two main reasons to avoid frequent small auto-grow events. One is that, as discussed in Chapter 7, log files cannot take advantage of instant file initialization, so each log growth event is relatively expensive, compared to data file growth, in terms of resources. A second is that a fragmented log can impede the performance of operations that read the log.

Many operations will need to read the transaction log, including:

- **Full, differential and log backups** – though only the latter will need to read substantial portions of the log.

- **Crash recovery process** – to reconcile the contents of data and log files, undoing the effects of any uncommitted transactions, and redoing the effects of any that were committed and hardened to the log, but not to the data files (see Chapter 1).

- **Transactional replication** – the transactional replication log reader reads the log when moving changes from the publisher to the distributor.

- **Database mirroring** – on the mirror database, the log gets read when transferring latest changes from the primary to the mirror.

- **Creating a database snapshot** – which requires the crash recovery process to run.

- **DBBC CHECKDB** – which creates a database snapshot when it runs.

- **Change Data Capture** – which uses the transactional replication log reader to track data changes.

Ultimately, the question of a "reasonable" number of VLFs in a log file will depend on the size of the log. In general, Microsoft regards more than about 200 VLFs as a possible cause for concern, but in a very big log file (say 500 GB) having only 200 VLFs could also be a problem, with the VLFs being too large and limiting space reuse.

Transaction Log VLFs – too many or too few?

Kimberly Tripp's article discusses this topic in more detail:
HTTP://WWW.SQLSKILLS.COM/BLOGS/KIMBERLY/post/Transaction-Log-VLFs-too-many-or-too-few.aspx.

In order to get at least some idea of the size of the impact of a fragmented log on operations that need to read it, we'll run some tests to look at the impact on two processes that read the log extensively, namely **log backups** and the **crash recovery process**.

***

Disclaimer

The tests that follow in no way reflect the reality of busy multi-user databases running on server-grade hardware, with specific RAID configurations and so on. We ran them on an isolated SQL Server 2008 instance, installed on a virtual machine. Your figures are likely to vary, and the observed impact will obviously be lower for faster disks. The idea is simply to offer some insight into potential log fragmentation issues, and some pointers on how to investigate their potential impact.

***

Note, finally, that Linchi Shea has demonstrated a big effect on the performance of data modifications when comparing a database with 20,000 VLFs to one with 16 VLFs. See: HTTP://SQLBLOG.COM/BLOGS/LINCHI_SHEA/ARCHIVE/2009/02/09/PERFORMANCE-IMPACT-A-LARGE-NUMBER-OF-VIRTUAL-LOG-FILES-PART-1.ASPX.

Effect on log backups

In order to get some idea of the size of the impact of a fragmented log on a log backup, we'll create `PersonsLots` database, and deliberately create a small log file (2 MB) and force it to grow in very small increments to create a very fragmented log. We'll load some data, run a big update to generate many log records, and then perform a log backup and see how long it takes. We'll then run a similar test on a database where we've pre-sized the log file correctly. You will find the full code for each test in the code download files **PersonsLots_LogBackupTest.sql** and **Persons_LogBackupTest.sql**.

First, we create the `PersonsLots` database. Its log file is only 2 MB in size and will auto-grow in 2 MB increments.

```
/*
mdf: initial size 195 MB, 16 MB growth
ldf: initial size 2 MB, 2 MB growth
*/

USE master
GO
IF DB_ID('PersonsLots') IS NOT NULL
    DROP DATABASE PersonsLots;
GO

-- Clear backup history
EXEC msdb.dbo.sp_delete_database_backuphistory @database_name = N'PersonsLots'
GO

CREATE DATABASE [PersonsLots] ON PRIMARY
 (    NAME = N'PersonsLots'
    , FILENAME = N'C:\SQLData\PersonsLots.mdf'
    , SIZE = 199680KB
    , FILEGROWTH = 16384KB
 )
 LOG ON
 (    NAME = N'PersonsLots_log'
    , FILENAME = N'D:\SQLData\PersonsLots_log.ldf'
    , SIZE = 2048KB
    , FILEGROWTH = 2048KB
 )
GO

ALTER DATABASE PersonsLots SET RECOVERY FULL;

USE master
GO
BACKUP DATABASE PersonsLots
TO DISK ='D:\SQLBackups\PersonsLots_full.bak'
WITH INIT;
GO
```

```
DBCC SQLPERF(LOGSPACE) ;
--2 MB, 15% used
USE Persons
GO
DBCC LOGINFO;
-- 4 VLFs
```

Listing 8.4:   Create the `PersonsLots` database.

Now, we're going to grow the log in lots of very small increments, as shown in Listing 8.5, in order to produce a very fragmented log file.

```
DECLARE @LogGrowth INT = 0;
DECLARE @sSQL NVARCHAR(4000)
WHILE @LogGrowth < 4096

BEGIN

        SET @sSQL = 'ALTER DATABASE PersonsLots
                    MODIFY FILE (NAME = PersonsLots_log,
                    SIZE = ' + CAST(4096+2048*@LogGrowth AS VARCHAR(10))
                                                    + 'KB );'
        EXEC(@sSQL);
        SET @LogGrowth = @LogGrowth + 1;
END
USE PersonsLots
GO
DBCC LOGINFO
--16388 VLFs

DBCC SQLPERF (LOGSPACE);
-- 8194 MB, 6.3% full
```

Listing 8.5:   Creating a very fragmented log for `PersonsLots`.

Here we grow the log in 4,096 increments to a total size of 8 GB
(4096+2048*4096 KB). The log will grow 4,096 times, adding 4 VLFs
each time for a grand total of 4+(4096*4) = 16388 VLFs.

Now rerun Listing 8.2 to re-create the **Persons** table, but this time in the **PersonsLots** database, and then adapt Listing 8.3 to populate the table with 1 million rows. Now we're going to update the **Persons** table to create many log records. Depending on the specs of your machine, you may have time for a cup of coffee while Listing 8.6 runs.

```
USE PersonsLots
GO
/* this took 6 mins*/
DECLARE @cnt INT;

SET @cnt = 1;

WHILE @cnt < 6
    BEGIN;
        SET @cnt = @cnt + 1;
        UPDATE   dbo.Persons
        SET      Email = LEFT(Email + Email, 7000)
    END;

DBCC SQLPERF(LOGSPACE) ;
--8194 MB, 67% used
DBCC LOGINFO;
-- 16388 VLFs
```

Listing 8.6:   A big update on the **Persons** table.

Finally, we're ready to take a log backup and see how long it takes. We've included the backup statistics in a comment after the backup code.

```
USE master
GO
BACKUP LOG PersonsLots
TO DISK ='D:\SQLBackups\PersonsLots_log.trn'
WITH INIT;

/*Processed 666930 pages for database 'PersonsLots', file 'PersonsLots_log' on file
1.
BACKUP LOG successfully processed 666930 pages in 123.263 seconds (42.270 MB/
sec).*/
```

Listing 8.7: Log backup of `PersonsLots` (fragmented log).

For comparison, we'll repeat the same test, but this time we'll carefully size our database log to have a reasonable number of reasonably sized VLFs. In Listing 8.8, we re-create the **Persons** database, with an initial log size of 2 GB (= 16 VLFs, each 128 MB in size). We then manually grow the log, just three steps to 8 GB in size, comprising 64 VLFs (each roughly 128 MB in size).

```
USE master
GO
IF DB_ID('Persons') IS NOT NULL
    DROP DATABASE Persons;
GO

CREATE DATABASE [Persons] ON PRIMARY
 (   NAME = N'Persons'
   , FILENAME = N'C:\SQLData\Persons.mdf'
   , SIZE = 2097152KB
   , FILEGROWTH = 1048576KB
 )
 LOG ON
 (   NAME = N'Persons_log'
   , FILENAME = N'D:\SQLData\Persons_log.ldf'
   , SIZE = 2097152KB
   , FILEGROWTH = 2097152KB
 )
GO
```

```
USE Persons
GO
DBCC LOGINFO;
-- 16 VLFs

USE master
GO
ALTER DATABASE Persons MODIFY FILE ( NAME = N'Persons_log', SIZE = 4194304KB )
GO
-- 32 VLFs

ALTER DATABASE Persons MODIFY FILE ( NAME = N'Persons_log', SIZE = 6291456KB )
GO
-- 48 VLFs

ALTER DATABASE Persons MODIFY FILE ( NAME = N'Persons_log', SIZE = 8388608KB )
GO
-- 64 VLFs

ALTER DATABASE Persons SET RECOVERY FULL;

USE master
GO
BACKUP DATABASE Persons
TO DISK ='D:\SQLBackups\Persons_full.bak'
WITH INIT;
GO
```

Listing 8.8: Create the Persons database and manually grow the log.

Now rerun Listings 8.2, 8.3 (with 1 million rows) and 8.6 exactly as for the previous test. You should find that, in the absence of any log growth events, Listing 8.6 runs a lot quicker (in half the time, in our tests). Finally, rerun a log backup.

```
USE master
GO
BACKUP LOG Persons
TO DISK ='D:\SQLBackups\Persons_log.trn'
WITH INIT;

/*Processed 666505 pages for database 'Persons', file 'Persons_log' on file 1.
BACKUP LOG successfully processed 666505 pages in 105.706 seconds (49.259 MB/sec).
*/
```

Listing 8.9: Log backup of the `Persons` database (non-fragmented log).

The effect on log backup time is relatively small, but reproducible, for this sized log, about a 15–20% increase in backup time for a log with 14,292 VLFs compared to one with 64, and of course, this is a relatively small database (albeit with a very heavily fragmented log).

Effect on crash recovery

In these tests, we investigate the effect of log fragmentation on crash recovery, since this process will require SQL Server to read the active log and redo or undo log records as necessary in order to return the database to a consistent state.

Lots of redo

In the first example, we reuse the `PersonsLots` database. Drop and re-create it, set the recovery model to `FULL`, take a full backup and then insert 1 million rows, as per previous listings. You can find the full code for the examples in this section in the files, **PersonsLots_RedoTest.sql** and **Persons_RedoTest.sql**, as part of the code download for this book.

Now, before we update these rows, we're going to disable automatic checkpoints.

> ***Never disable automatic checkpoints!***
>
> *We're doing so here purely for the purposes of this test. It is **not** something that we in any way*
> *recommend during normal operation of a SQL Server database.*
> *See:* HTTP://SUPPORT.MICROSOFT.COM/KB/815436 *for more details.*

When we commit the subsequent updates, we'll immediately shut down the database so that all of the updates are hardened to the log but not to the data file. Therefore, during crash recovery, SQL Server will need to read all of the related log records and redo all of the operations.

```
USE PersonsLots
Go
/*Disable Automatic checkpoints*/
DBCC TRACEON( 3505 )

/*Turn the flag off once the test is complete!*/
--DBCC TRACEOFF (3505)

/* this took 5 mins*/
BEGIN TRANSACTION
DECLARE @cnt INT;

SET @cnt = 1;

WHILE @cnt < 6
    BEGIN;
        SET @cnt = @cnt + 1;
        UPDATE  dbo.Persons
        SET     Email = LEFT(Email + Email, 7000)
    END;

DBCC SQLPERF(LOGSPACE) ;
--11170 MB, 100% used
USE PersonsLots
GO
DBCC LOGINFO;
-- 22340 VLFs
```

Listing 8.10: `PersonsLots` – disable automatic checkpoints and run update in an explicit transaction.

Now we commit the transaction and shut down.

```
/*Commit and immediately shut down*/
COMMIT TRANSACTION;
SHUTDOWN WITH NOWAIT
```

Listing 8.11:   Commit the transaction and shut down SQL Server.

After restarting the SQL Server service, try to access **PersonsLots**, and you'll see a message stating that it is in recovery.

```
USE PersonsLots
Go
/*Msg 922, Level 14, State 2, Line 1
Database 'PersonsLots' is being recovered. Waiting until recovery is finished.*/
```

Listing 8.12:   PersonsLots is undergoing a recovery operation.

SQL Server has to open the log and read each VLF before it starts recovering the database. So the impact of many VLFs is that it could extend the time between SQL Server restarting the database, and the actual start of the recovery process.

Therefore, once the database is accessible, we can interrogate the error log for time between these two events, as well as the total recovery time.

```
EXEC sys.xp_readerrorlog 0, 1, 'PersonsLots'

/*
2012-10-03 11:28:14.240   Starting up database 'PersonsLots'.
2012-10-03 11:28:26.710   Recovery of database 'PersonsLots' (6) is 0%
                          complete (approximately 155 seconds remain).
2012-10-03 11:28:33.000   140 transactions rolled forward in database
                          'PersonsLots' (6).
2012-10-03 11:28:33.010   Recovery completed for database PersonsLots
                          (database ID 6) in 6 second(s)
                          (analysis 2238 ms, redo 4144 ms, undo 12 ms.)
*/
```

Listing 8.13:   Interrogate the error log for PersonsLots messages.

There were approximately 12.5 seconds between SQL Server starting up the database, and the start of the recovery process. This is why it's possible to see a database listed as "in recovery," without initially seeing any recovery messages in the error log. The recovery process then took under 7 seconds. Notice that, of the three recovery phases, SQL Server spent most time in redo.

Let's now repeat the same test with the **Persons** database (pre-sized log file).

```
USE Persons
Go
/*Disable Automatic checkpoints*/
DBCC TRACEON( 3505 )
--DBCC TRACEOFF (3505)

USE Persons
Go
BEGIN TRANSACTION
DECLARE @cnt INT;

SET @cnt = 1;

WHILE @cnt < 6
    BEGIN;
        SET @cnt = @cnt + 1;
        UPDATE   dbo.Persons
        SET      Email = LEFT(Email + Email, 7000)
    END;

DBCC SQLPERF(LOGSPACE) ;
-- 12288 MB, 87.2% used
USE Persons
GO
DBCC LOGINFO;
-- 96 VLFs

/*Commit and immediately Shut down*/
COMMIT TRANSACTION;
SHUTDOWN WITH NOWAIT
```

Listing 8.14: Persons: disable automatic checkpoints, run and commit explicit transaction, shut down SQL Server.

Finally, we interrogate the error log again, for time between these two events, as well as the total recovery time.

```
EXEC sys.xp_readerrorlog 0, 1, 'Persons'

/*
2012-10-03 11:54:21.410   Starting up database 'Persons'.
2012-10-03 11:54:21.890   Recovery of database 'Persons' (6) is 0%
                          complete (approximately 108 seconds remain).
2012-10-03 11:54:30.690   1 transactions rolled forward in database
                          'Persons' (6).
2012-10-03 11:54:30.710   Recovery completed for database Persons
                          (database ID 6) in 3 second(s)
                          (analysis 2177 ms, redo 1058 ms, undo 10 ms.)
*/
```

Listing 8.15: Interrogate the error log for `Persons` messages.

Note that, this time, there is less than 0.5 seconds between SQL Server starting up the database, and recovery beginning. The recovery process took just over 9 seconds.

You will see that in these tests we haven't created a situation in which all other things are equal, aside from the log fragmentation. For a start, the recovery process for the fragmented log database rolls forward 140 transactions, and in the second test, only rolls forward 1 transaction.

However, it is clear from the tests that a fragmented log can significantly delay the onset of the actual database recovery process, while SQL Server reads in all of the VLFs.

Lots of undo

As an alternative example, we could execute our long update transaction, run a checkpoint and then shut down SQL Server with the transaction uncommitted, and see how long SQL Server takes to recover the database, first when the log is fragmented and then when it is not. In each case, this will force SQL Server to perform a lot of undo in order to perform recovery, and we'll see the effect, if any, of an internally fragmented log.

We won't show the full code for these tests here as we've presented it all previously, but it's available in the code download files for this book (see **PersonsLots_UndoTest.sql** and **Persons_UndoTest.sql**).

```
/* (1) Recreate PersonsLots, with a fragmented log (Listing 8.4 and 8.5)
   (2) Create Persons table, Insert 1 million rows (Listings 8.2 and 8.3)
*/

BEGIN TRANSACTION

/* run update from Listing 8.6*/

/*Force a checkpoint*/
CHECKPOINT;

/*In an second session, immediately Shutdown without commiting*/
SHUTDOWN WITH NOWAIT
```

Listing 8.16:   The "lots of undo" test on `PersonsLots` (fragmented log).

Repeat the same test for the `Persons` database (as defined in **Persons_UndoTest.sql**). Listing 8.17 shows the results from the error logs for each database.

```
/*
PersonsLots (fragmented log)

2012-10-03 12:51:35.360   Starting up database 'PersonsLots'.
2012-10-03 12:51:46.920   Recovery of database 'PersonsLots' (17) is 0%
                          complete (approximately 10863 seconds remain).
2012-10-03 12:57:12.680   1 transactions rolled back in database
                          'PersonsLots' (17).
2012-10-03 12:57:14.680   Recovery completed for database PersonsLots
                          (database ID 17) in 326 second(s)
                          (analysis 30 ms, redo 78083 ms, undo 246689 ms.)


Persons (non-fragmented log)

2012-10-03 13:21:23.250   Starting up database 'Persons'.
2012-10-03 13:21:23.740   Recovery of database 'Persons' (6) is 0%
                          complete (approximately 10775 seconds remain).
2012-10-03 13:26:03.840   1 transactions rolled back in database
                          'Persons' (6).
2012-10-03 13:26:03.990   Recovery completed for database Persons
                          (database ID 6) in 279 second(s)
                          (analysis 24 ms, redo 57468 ms, undo 221671 ms.)
*/
```

Listing 8.17:   Error log database startup and recovery information for PersonsLots and Persons.

For PersonsLots the delay between database startup and the start of recovery is over 11 seconds, whereas for Persons it is about 0.5 seconds.

The overall recovery times are much longer in these undo examples, compared to the previous redo examples. For PersonsLots, the total recovery time was 326 seconds, compared to 279 seconds for Persons, with the non-fragmented log.

Correct Log Sizing

We hope that the previous examples in this chapter demonstrate clearly that it is a very bad idea to undersize the transaction log and then allow it to grow in small increments. In addition, it is usually a bad idea to accept the auto-growth settings that a database will inherit from `model`, which is currently to grow in steps of 10% of the current transaction log size, for the reasons below.

- **Initially, when the log file is small**, the incremental growth will be small, resulting in the creation of a large number of small VLFs in the log, causing the fragmentation issues discussed earlier.

- **When the log file is very large**, the growth increments will be correspondingly large. Since the transaction log has to be zeroed out during initialization, large growth events can take time and, if the log can't be grown fast enough, this can result in 9002 (transaction log full) errors and even in the auto-grow timing out and being rolled back.

The way to avoid issues relating to expensive log growth events and log fragmentation, is simply to set the correct initial size for the log file, allowing for current requirements, and predicted growth over a set period.

Ideally, having done this, the log would never auto-grow, which isn't to say that we should disable the auto-growth facility. It must be there as a safety mechanism, but we should size the log appropriately so that we are not relying on auto-growth being the mechanism that controls log growth. We can configure the auto-growth settings explicitly to a fixed size that allows the log file to grow quickly if necessary, while also minimizing the number of VLFs SQL Server adds to the log file for each growth event. As discussed previously, auto-growth events are expensive, due to zero-initialization. In order to minimize the chances of a time-out occurring during auto-growth, it's a good idea to measure how long it takes to grow the transaction log by a variety of set sizes, while the database is operating under normal workload, and based on the current I/O subsystem configuration.

So, how do we size the log correctly? There is no easy answer. There is no sound logic behind suggestions such as "The log should be at least 25% of the size of the database." We must simply pick a reasonable size based on the following considerations, and then track log growth.

- **Log must be big enough to accommodate largest single transaction**, for example the largest index rebuild. This means the log must be bigger than the largest index in the database, to allow for logging requirements to rebuild the index under FULL recovery, and must be big enough to accommodate all activity that might occur concurrently while that largest transaction is running.

- **Log sizing must account for how much log is generated between log backups** (e.g. in 30 minutes, or 1 hour).

- **Log sizing must account for any processes that may delay truncation**, such as replication, where the log reader agent job may only run once per hour.

We must also remember to factor in log reservation. The logging subsystem reserves space when logging a transaction to ensure that the log can't run out of space during a rollback. As such, the required log space is actually greater than the total size of log records for the operation.

In short, a rollback operation logs **compensation log records**, and if a rollback were to run out of log space, SQL Server would have to be mark the database as suspect. This log reservation is not actually "used" log space, it's just a specific amount of space that must remain free, but it can trigger auto-growth events if the log fills to a point where the "used space + reserved space = log size," and it is counted as used space for the purposes of DBCC SQLPERF(LOGSPACE).

Hence, it is possible to see the space used reported by DBCC SQLPERF(LOGSPACE) drop after a transaction commits, even if the database is in FULL recovery model, and no log backup has run. To see this in action, we just need a FULL recovery model database with a table containing about 50K rows. We won't repeat the full code for that here, but it's included in the code download (**Persons_LogReservation.sql**).

```
BACKUP LOG Persons
TO DISK='D:\SQLBackups\Persons_log.trn'
WITH INIT;

-- start a transaction
BEGIN TRANSACTION

DBCC SQLPERF(LOGSPACE)
/*LogSize: 34 MB ; Log Space Used: 12%*/

-- update the Persons table
UPDATE   dbo.Persons
SET      email = ' __ '

DBCC SQLPERF(LOGSPACE)
/*LogSize: 34 MB ; Log Space Used: 87%*/

COMMIT TRANSACTION

DBCC SQLPERF(LOGSPACE)
/*LogSize: 34 MB ; Log Space Used: 34%*/
```

Listing 8.18: Log reservation test.

Note that the log space used has dropped from 87% to 34%, even though this is a FULL recovery model database, and there was no log backup after the transaction committed. SQL Server has not truncated the log in this case, merely released the log reservation space, after the transaction committed.

Having set the initial log size, based on all of these requirements, and set a sensible auto-growth safety net, it's wise to monitor log usage, and set alerts for log auto-growth events, since, if we've done our job properly, they should be rare. Chapter 9 will discuss log monitoring in more detail.

What To Do If Things Go Wrong

In this final section, we'll consider appropriate action in the face of a bloated and fragmented log file. Perhaps a database only recently fell under our care; we've implemented some monitoring and realized that the log is almost full and that there isn't the capacity on its disk drive to accommodate an urgent index maintenance operation. We try a log backup but, for reasons we need to investigate further (see Chapter 7), SQL Server will not truncate the log. In order to buy some time, we add a secondary log file, on a separate disk, and the operation proceeds as planned.

We investigate why the log ballooned in size and it turns out to be an application leaving "orphaned transactions" in the database. The issue is fixed, and the next log backup truncates the log, creating plenty of reusable space.

The next question is "what next?" given that we now have a database with multiple log files and a principal log file that is bloated and likely to be highly fragmented.

The first point is that we want to get rid of that secondary log file as soon as possible. As noted previously, there is no performance advantage to having multiple log files and, now that it's no longer required, all it will really do is slow down any restore operations, since SQL Server has to zero-initialize the log during full and differential restore operations.

Run Listing 8.4 to re-create the `PersonsLots` database, followed by Listings 8.2 and 8.3 to create and populate the `Persons` table (we provide the complete script, **PersonsLots_2logs.sql**, in the code download).

Let's assume, at this point, the DBA adds a second 3-GB log file to accommodate database maintenance operations.

```
USE master
GO
ALTER DATABASE PersonsLots
ADD LOG FILE ( NAME = N'PersonsLots_Log2',
FILENAME = N'D:\SQLData\Persons_lots2.ldf' , SIZE = 3146000KB , FILEGROWTH =
314600KB )
GO
```

Listing 8.19: Adding a 3-GB secondary log file to `PersonsLots`.

Some time later, we've fixed the problem that resulted in delayed log truncation; there is now plenty of reusable space in the primary log file, and we no longer need this secondary log file, but it still exists. Let's restore the `PersonsLots` database.

```
USE master
GO
RESTORE DATABASE PersonsLots
FROM DISK ='D:\SQLBackups\PersonsLots_full.bak'
WITH NORECOVERY;

RESTORE DATABASE PersonsLots
FROM DISK='D:\SQLBackups\PersonsLots.trn'
WITH Recovery;

/*<output truncated>...
Processed 18094 pages for database 'PersonsLots', file 'PersonsLots_log' on file 1.
Processed 0 pages for database 'PersonsLots', file 'PersonsLots_Log2' on file 1.
RESTORE LOG successfully processed 18094 pages in 62.141 seconds (2.274 MB/sec).*/
```

Listing 8.20: Restoring `PersonsLots` (with secondary log file).

The restore took over 60 seconds. If we repeat the exact same steps, but without adding the secondary log file, the comparative restore, in our tests, took about 8 seconds.

In order to remove the secondary log file, we need to wait until it contains no part of the active log. Since our goal is to remove it, it's permissible to shrink this secondary log file to zero (demonstrated shortly), and turn off auto-growth for this file, as this will "encourage" the active log to move swiftly back into the primary log file. It's important to note that this will *not* move any log records in the secondary log over to the primary log. (Some people expect this behavior because, if we specify the **EMPTYFILE** parameter when shrinking a data file, SQL Server will move the data to another data file in the same filegroup.)

Once the secondary log file contains no part of the active log, we can simply remove it.

```
USE PersonsLots
GO
ALTER DATABASE PersonsLots  REMOVE FILE PersonsLots_Log2
GO
```

Listing 8.21:   Removing the secondary log file.

This is one problem solved, but we may still have a bloated and fragmented primary log. While we should never shrink the log as part of our standard maintenance operations, as discussed in Chapter 7, it is permissible in situations such as this, in the knowledge that we have investigated and resolved the cause of the excessive log growth, and so shrinking the log should be a "one-off" event.

The recommended approach is to use **DBCC SHRINKFILE** (see HTTP://MSDN.MICROSOFT. COM/EN-US/LIBRARY/MS189493.ASPX) to reclaim the space. If we don't specify a target size, or if we specify 0 (zero) as the target size, we can shrink the log back to its original size (in this case, 2 MB) and minimize fragmentation of the log file. If the initial size of the log was large, we wish to shrink the log smaller than this, in which case we specify a `target_size`, such as "1".

```
USE PersonsLots
GO
DBCC SHRINKFILE (N'PersonsLots_log' , target_size=0)
GO
```

	DbId	FileId	Current Size	Minimum Size	Used Pages	Estimated Pages
1	18	2	24128	256	24128	256

Listing 8.22: Shrinking the primary log file (partial success).

In the output from this command, we see the current database size (24128*8-KB pages) and minimum possible size after shrinking (256*8-KB pages). This is actually an indication that the shrink did not work fully. SQL Server shrank the log to the point where the last VLF in the file contained part of the active log, and then stopped. Check the messages tab for confirmation.

```
/*Cannot shrink log file 2 (PersonsLots_log) because the logical log file located
at the end of the file is in use.

(1 row(s) affected)
DBCC execution completed. If DBCC printed error messages, contact your system
administrator.*/
Perform a log backup and try again.


USE master
GO
BACKUP DATABASE PersonsLots
TO DISK ='D:\SQLBackups\PersonsLots_full.bak'
WITH INIT;
GO

BACKUP LOG PersonsLots
TO DISK = 'D:\SQLBackups\PersonsLots.trn'
WITH init
```

```
USE PersonsLots
GO
DBCC SHRINKFILE (N'PersonsLots_log' , 0)
GO
```

	DbId	FileId	Current Size	Minimum Size	Used Pages	Estimated Pages
1	18	2	256	256	256	256

Listing 8.23: Shrinking the primary log file after log backup.

Having done this, we can now manually grow the log to the required size, as demonstrated previously in Listing 8.8.

Summary

We started with a brief overview of the physical architecture factors that can affect log throughput, such as the need to separate log file I/O onto a dedicated array, and choose the optimal RAID level for this array.

This chapter then emphasized the need to manage transaction log growth explicitly, rather than let SQL Server auto-growth events "manage" it for us. If we undersize the log initially, and then let SQL Server auto-grow it in small increments, we'll end up with a fragmented log. Examples in the chapter demonstrated how this might affect the performance of any SQL Server operations that need to read the log.

Finally, we discussed the factors that determine the correct log size, and correct auto-growth increment for a given database, and we offered advice on how to recover from a situation where a database suffers from multiple log files and an oversized and fragmented primary log.

The next chapter, the final one in this book, will describe the various tools and techniques for monitoring log activity, throughput, and fragmentation.

Further Reading

- Manage the Size of the Transaction Log File
  HTTP://MSDN.MICROSOFT.COM/EN-US/LIBRARY/MS365418.ASPX

- The Trouble with Transaction Logs
  HTTP://THOMASLAROCK.COM/2012/08/THE-TROUBLE-WITH-TRANSACTION-LOGS/

- How to shrink the SQL Server log
  HTTP://RUSANU.COM/2012/07/27/HOW-TO-SHRINK-THE-SQL-SERVER-LOG/

- Multiple log files and why they're bad
  HTTP://WWW.SQLSKILLS.COM/BLOGS/PAUL/POST/Multiple-log-files-and-why-theyre-bad.aspx

Acknowledgements

Many thanks to Jonathan Kehayias, who contributed the RAID section of this chapter.

Chapter 9: Monitoring the Transaction Log

Our major goal in terms of log maintenance for all databases under our care is to optimize for write performance, in order to support all activities that require SQL Server to write to the log, including data modifications, data loads, index rebuilds, and so on. However, it's also important to keep an eye on possible log fragmentation, which, as described previously, can affect the performance of processes that need to read the log, such as log backups and the crash recovery process.

Having configured the physical log architecture, and sized the log file appropriately, as discussed in the previous chapter, this chapter describes some of the ways in which we can monitor transaction log size, growth and activity, in order to receive immediate warning of unexpected or explosive log growth, log fragmentation, and so on.

Note that we do not intend this chapter to be comprehensive in its coverage of log monitoring solutions. For example, we offer no coverage of log monitoring using Extended Events, or the SQL Server Data Collector / Management Data Warehouse (available with SQL Server 2008 and later). See the *Further Reading* section at the end of this chapter, for some links to these topics.

However, we have tried to cover the most common monitoring tools and techniques, including:

- **Monitoring tools** – looking briefly at Windows Performance Monitor and Red Gate SQL Monitor.

- **Using the Dynamic Management Objects** – to investigate log activity at the server, file or database level.

- **Using T-SQL or PowerShell scripting** – to report log characteristics and usage across all servers.

Monitoring Tools

Several tools are available that will, among other things, allow us to monitor activity on our database files, including the log. Here, we'll consider just two in brief; a built-in tool (Perfmon) and a third-party tool (Red Gate SQL Monitor).

Windows Perfmon

A popular "built-in" tool for monitoring SQL Server activity is Windows Performance Monitor (Perfmon). It is a Windows OS monitoring tool that provides a vast range of counters for monitoring memory, disk I/O, CPU and network usage on a server (for example, see HTTP://TECHNET.MICROSOFT.COM/EN-US/LIBRARY/CC768048.ASPX), and also exposes the counters maintained by SQL Server. Generally, the DBA or system administrator would set up Perfmon to record statistics from various counters at regular intervals, storing the data in a file and then importing it into Excel, or a similar tool, for analysis.

Amongst its many counters, it offers a number to measure disk read and write performance, as well as specific counters for log monitoring.

There are plenty of available tutorials on the use of Perfmon, and we won't repeat those in any detail here. In addition to documentation on TechNet (HTTP://TECHNET.MICROSOFT.COM/EN-US/LIBRARY/CC749249.ASPX), we recommend the articles below for those new to this tool.

- **SQL Server Perfmon Best Practices, by Brent Ozar**
  A comprehensive tutorial on use of the tools and recommended counters for monitoring SQL Server, and how to analyze the saved data in Excel.
  HTTP://WWW.BRENTOZAR.COM/ARCHIVE/2006/12/
  DBA-101-USING-PERFMON-FOR-SQL-PERFORMANCE-TUNING/

- **Correlating SQL Server Profiler with Performance Monitor, by BradMcGehee**
  A "quick start" tutorial on use of Perfmon, plus how to correlate Perfmon data with
  Profiler trace data.
  HTTP://WWW.SIMPLE-TALK.COM/SQL/DATABASE-ADMINISTRATION/
  CORRELATING-SQL-SERVER-PROFILER-WITH-PERFORMANCE-MONITOR/

- **Baselining and Benchmarking, by Brent Ozar**
  A video tutorial providing an overview of monitoring using Performance Monitor, and
  Profiler, as well as benchmarking "whys" and "hows."
  HTTP://TECHNET.MICROSOFT.COM/EN-US/SQLSERVER/GG429821.ASPX

In terms of the general performance of the disks housing the log (and data) files, we can
monitor the following pairs of counters:

- **Physical Disk\Disk Reads/sec** and **Physical Disk\Disk Writes/sec** – we
  need to know the values of these counters and, having established a baseline, look out
  for marked rises in either, and investigate their cause.

- **Physical Disk\Avg. Disk sec/Read** and **Physical Disk\Avg. Disk sec/Write**
  – the average times (in ms) of a read and write to disk; these counters provide the **disk
  latency** stats that can be used to pinpoint potential I/O bottlenecks.

Popular guideline values for the disk latency counters suggest that less than 10 ms is
"good," anything over 20–30 ms is "OK" but potentially worrying, and anything over about
50 ms indicates a possible I/O bottleneck. Of course, these figures are entirely dependent
on the specification and configuration of the disk array in your environment.

For a very simple demo of Perfmon in action, we'll just set it up to monitor counter
activity for the Physical Disk\Avg. Disk sec/Read and Physical Disk\Avg. Disk
sec/Write counters whilst one of the databases is under a heavy write load.

For our examples, we're going to re-create a new version of the **Persons** database and table from Chapter 8. In the code download for this chapter, the script, **Ch09_Persons.sql** re-creates the **Persons** database, in FULL recovery model, followed by the **Persons** table. It then populates the table with 1 million rows of data (from the **AdventureWorks2008** database, though it will also work with **AdventureWorks2012**).

We can now start Windows Perfmon (just search for "perfmon" from the Start menu). If you just want to see an instant snapshot of certain activity, you can simply add counters directly to the Perfmon graph. However, if you wish to define a particular set on counters to monitor over time, on a schedule, then you'll need to define a new data collection set. Under **Data Collector Sets**, right-click on **User Defined** and select **New | Data Collector Set** (these data collector sets are unrelated to the SQL Server Data Collector mentioned in the introduction to this chapter).

Give your new Data Collector Set a name, and choose whether to select the counters based on a pre-supplied template or manually (I chose the latter for this simple example). At the next screen, opt to include only performance counter data, and at the one after, you get to select the performance counters.

Click **Add...**, type in the path to the appropriate server, hit the **Enter** key and wait a few seconds (or longer, sometimes!) while it connects and populates the box below with the available counters. You can now go through and add the ones you want. On this occasion, we're only interested in the **PhysicalDisk** class, so click on it to expand it and select the relevant counters.

Notice that we're monitoring the counters for two separate disk drives (the data file for the **Persons** database is on the **C:** drive and the log file on the **D:** drive), rather than capturing the total values for all drives. If both of these files are on the same drive, on your test machine, then you can simply collect the counters for the appropriate single drive.

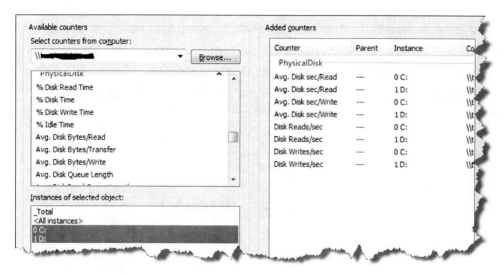

Figure 9.1: Setting up Perfmon.

Having clicked **OK**, we return to the previous screen and simply need to confirm the collection interval (this will vary, depending on what you're monitoring; I just chose one second for this simple example) and click **Finish**.

We can run this new data collection set on a schedule, of course, but here we'll simply right-click on it and select **Start** (after a second or two, a green "Play" symbol will appear). Back in SSMS, we create a reasonably heavy write load on our `Persons` database, as shown in Listing 9.1.

```
USE Persons
GO
DECLARE @cnt INT;

SET @cnt = 1;
-- may take several minutes; reduce the number of loops, if required
WHILE @cnt < 6
    BEGIN;
        SET @cnt = @cnt + 1;
        UPDATE   dbo.Persons
        SET      Email = LEFT(Email + Email, 7000)
    END;
```

Listing 9.1: Updating the `Persons` table.

Once the code completes, return to Perfmon, right-click on your data collector set and stop the data collection. Navigate to the **Reports** menu item and under **User Defined** you should find a list of reports, with names of the form **ClientName_Date_Number**. Locate the relevant report and double-click on it to view the data in graphical form, as shown in Figure 9.2.

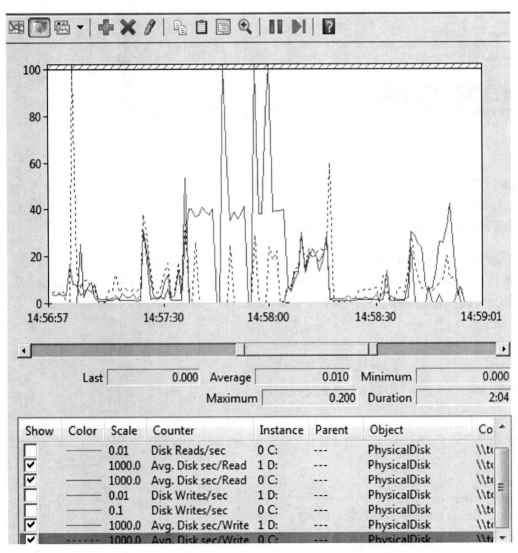

Figure 9.2:   A snapshot of disk read and write activity, using Perfmon.

You can select and deselect the counters you wish to display, and by double-clicking on any one, in the counter listing below the graph, you can modify their appearance on the graph, the scale, and so on. You can also zoom in to an area of the graph by clicking on the graph and dragging across to highlight the required area and then clicking the magnifying glass from the top menu (use the horizontal scroll bar directly below the graph to zoom back out).

The dominant activity on the graph is disk writes to the **D:** drive, hosting our log file. We can see that, for periods, the latency sits at around 40 ms, but with frequent higher spikes. We can use the **Change Graph type** icon from the top menu to view a report. Over the entire collection period, the report shows an average latency for writes to the **D:** drive of 55 ms, which could be a cause for concern if seen for sustained periods. Of course, many other **PhysicalDisk** counters, and other counters, are available that can offer insight into the underlying performance of your disks (`%DiskTime`, `DiskTransfers/sec` and so on), and we should undertake a deeper analysis before jumping to conclusions.

In addition, and in a similar manner, we could collect other log-related counters, such as those available in the `SQL Server:Databases` object. This object offers various counters for investigation of log activity, including among others (see HTTP://MSDN. MICROSOFT.COM/EN-US/LIBRARY/MS189883.ASPX):

- `Log File(s) Size (KB)` and `Log File(s) Used Size (KB)` – total size of transaction log and how much is currently being used.

- `Log Flushes/sec` and `Log Bytes Flushed/sec` – number and size of writes from log cache to disk.

Red Gate SQL Monitor

If you use a third-party SQL Server monitoring tool, it is highly likely that it will collect
and store for analysis many of these counter values. Figure 9.3 shows `Log File(s)`
`Size` values, in Red Gate's SQL Monitor tool, as the log file for the `Persons` database
undergoes rapid growth, because of an incorrectly sized and configured log.

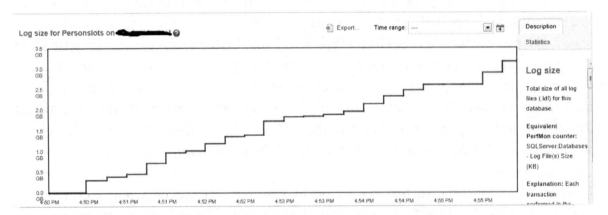

Figure 9.3:   Rapid log growth, as reported by SQL Monitor.

A nice feature of SQL Monitor is that it makes it very easy, much easier than with
Perfmon, to compare the same type of activity across different periods. In the **Time range**
drop-down, we can change the time range, set a custom range, as well as compare values
for this metric from today (or "this week") to those captured yesterday (or "last week"),
and so on.

Dynamic Management Views and Functions

Many DMVs (the generic acronym commonly used to refer collectively to Dynamic Management Views and Functions) offer insight into how the SQL Server engine uses the disk I/O subsystem, and the ability of that subsystem to cope with the I/O throughput and performance demanded by the system workload. For example:

- **sys.dm_io_virtual_file_stats** – provides statistics on utilization of all database data and log files. It is an excellent resource for discovering hot spots, and identifying opportunities to spread I/O over different channels.

- **sys.dm_io_pending_io_requests** – provides a list of all I/O operations that SQL Server is currently waiting to complete.

Dropping down to the operating system level, the "**sys.dm_os_**" category of DMVs provides a vast amount of detailed data regarding the nature of the interaction between SQL Server and the operating system. This gives us insight into how the workload represented by the submitted requests translates into actual work in the operating system. Notably, the **sys.dm_os_wait_stats** records the length of time waited, and the requested resource, every time a session has to wait before proceeding with its work. It's a very useful DMV for finding out what is causing sessions to wait, including, of course, I/O waits.

The "**sys.dm_os_**" category of DMVs also provides **sys.dm_os_performance_ counters**, which exposes the performance counters, and therefore the "queues" in our system. Via specific resource measurements such as disk writes/sec, processor queue lengths, available memory, and so on, it helps us pinpoint the places where there is a lot of demand for a given resource, and the reasons for the excessive demand.

Up at the database level, SQL Server 2012 adds the **sys.dm_db_log_space_usage** DMV, providing a very simple means to retrieve basic transaction log size and space usage data, similar to that returned by **DBCC SQLPERF(LOGSPACE)**.

Here, we'll examine just three examples, starting with sys.dm_db_log_space_usage and then moving on to sys.dm_io_virtual_file_stats and then sys.dm_os_performance_counters, to expose detailed information on log activity and growth.

Using sys.dm_db_log_space_usage (SQL Server 2012 only)

If you're using SQL Server 2012 already, then getting basic log size and space information is very easy, as shown in Listing 9.2. We ran this code on a Persons2012 database, identical to Persons, except for the name.

```
SELECT
  DB_NAME(database_id) AS DatabaseName ,
  database_id ,
  CAST(( total_log_size_in_bytes / 1048576.0 ) AS DECIMAL(10, 1))
                                              AS TotalLogSizeMB ,
  CAST(( used_log_space_in_bytes / 1048576.0 ) AS DECIMAL(10, 1))
                                              AS LogSpaceUsedMB ,
  CAST(used_log_space_in_percent AS DECIMAL(10, 1)) AS LogSpaceUsedPercent
FROM    sys.dm_db_log_space_usage;
```

	DatabaseName	database_id	TotalLogSizeMB	LogSpaceUsedMB	LogSpaceUsedPercent
1	Persons2012	7	372.0	168.9	45.4

Listing 9.2:   Log size and space used.

Using sys.dm_io_virtual_file_stats

For each database file that SQL Server uses, data files as well as log (and full text) files, the sys.dm_io_virtual_file_stats function gives cumulative physical I/O statistics, indicating how frequently the file has been used by the database for reads and writes since the server was last rebooted. It also provides a very useful metric in the form of the "I/O stall" time, which indicates the total amount of time that user processes have waited for I/O to be completed on the file in question. Note that this DMV measures physical I/O only. Logical IO operations that read from cached data will not show up here. The function accepts a `database_id` and a `file_id`, which we can use to investigate specific files or databases, or we can simply return the data for all files on the server.

In order to start with a clean slate, rerun the script **Persons.sql** to drop and re-create the `Persons` database and table, and populate it with 1 million rows and then run Listing 9.3 to capture into a temporary table some baseline data for the server.

```
SELECT    DB_NAME(mf.database_id) AS databaseName ,
          mf.physical_name ,
          divfs.num_of_reads ,
          divfs.num_of_bytes_read ,
          divfs.io_stall_read_ms ,
          divfs.num_of_writes ,
          divfs.num_of_bytes_written ,
          divfs.io_stall_write_ms ,
          divfs.io_stall ,
          size_on_disk_bytes ,
          GETDATE() AS baselineDate
INTO      #baseline
FROM      sys.dm_io_virtual_file_stats(NULL, NULL) AS divfs
          JOIN sys.master_files AS mf ON mf.database_id = divfs.database_id
                                      AND mf.file_id = divfs.file_id
```

Listing 9.3:   Capturing baseline disk I/O statistics from `sys.dm_io_virtual_file_stats`
in a temporary table.

Listing 9.4 shows a query against the #baseline table, returning some the read and write statistics for the Persons database.

```
SELECT   physical_name ,
         num_of_reads ,
         num_of_bytes_read ,
         io_stall_read_ms ,
         num_of_writes ,
         num_of_bytes_written ,
         io_stall_write_ms
FROM     #baseline
WHERE    databaseName = 'Persons'
```

	physical_name	num_of_reads	num_of_bytes_read	io_stall_read_ms	num_of_writes	num_of_bytes_written	io_stall_write_ms
1	C:\SQLData\Persons.mdf	89	6971392	251	21	180224	26
2	D:\SQLData\Persons_log.ldf	21	455680	0	3250	198411776	16899

Listing 9.4: Querying the #baseline temporary table.

As noted, the data provided by this function is cumulative from when the server last restarted; in other words, the values in the data columns increment continuously, from the point when the server was last restarted. As such, a single "snapshot" of the data is rather meaningless, on its own. What we need to do is take a "baseline" measurement, wait for a set period, perhaps while a specific set of operations completes, then take a second measurement and subtract the two, so that you can see where I/O is "accumulating."

Rerun Listing 9.1 to update our **Persons** table, and run Listing 9.5 to collect a second set of data and subtract the baseline data values (we have omitted a few columns from the output, due purely to space constraints).

```
WITH  currentLine
      AS ( SELECT   DB_NAME(mf.database_id) AS databaseName ,
                    mf.physical_name ,
                    num_of_reads ,
                    num_of_bytes_read ,
                    io_stall_read_ms ,
                    num_of_writes ,
                    num_of_bytes_written ,
                    io_stall_write_ms ,
                    io_stall ,
                    size_on_disk_bytes ,
                    GETDATE() AS currentlineDate
           FROM     sys.dm_io_virtual_file_stats(NULL, NULL) AS divfs
                    JOIN sys.master_files AS mf
                      ON mf.database_id = divfs.database_id
                         AND mf.file_id = divfs.file_id
         )
SELECT  currentLine.databaseName ,
        LEFT(currentLine.physical_name, 1) AS drive ,
        currentLine.physical_name ,
        DATEDIFF(millisecond,baseLineDate,currentLineDate) AS elapsed_ms,
        currentLine.io_stall - #baseline.io_stall AS io_stall_ms ,
        currentLine.io_stall_read_ms - #baseline.io_stall_read_ms
                                               AS io_stall_read_ms ,
        currentLine.io_stall_write_ms - #baseline.io_stall_write_ms
                                               AS io_stall_write_ms ,
        currentLine.num_of_reads - #baseline.num_of_reads AS num_of_reads ,
        currentLine.num_of_bytes_read - #baseline.num_of_bytes_read
                                               AS num_of_bytes_read ,
        currentLine.num_of_writes - #baseline.num_of_writes AS num_of_writes ,
        currentLine.num_of_bytes_written - #baseline.num_of_bytes_written
                                               AS num_of_bytes_written
FROM  currentLine
    INNER JOIN #baseline ON #baseLine.databaseName = currentLine.databaseName
    AND #baseLine.physical_name = currentLine.physical_name
WHERE #baseline.databaseName = 'Persons' ;
```

	databaseName	drive	physical_name	io_stall_ms	io_stall_write_ms	num_of_writes	num_of_bytes_written
1	Persons	C	C:\SQLData\Persons.mdf	239205	160741	8455	1897177088
2	Persons	D	D:\SQLData\Persons_log.ldf	766202	766185	98147	6010466816

Listing 9.5:   Capturing disk I/O statistics, since the baseline measurement.

Clearly we forced some very heavy write activity on the log file in this example! Pinpointing the cause of high I/O stalls, and resolving the problem, is sometimes a complex process. If you suspect that I/O stall rates are causing issues, then the first course of action might be attempt to reduce the overall I/O load to acceptable levels. For example, we can use data from the execution- and index-related DMVs to attempt to reduce the overall I/O load on the server through tuning and indexing. We could also increase the amount of RAM, so that more data can be held in the data cache, and so reducing the occurrence of physical file reads. Armed with the I/O stall rate, and the amount of data read and written, we can also identify opportunities to implement partitioning, or to at least separate tables onto different filegroups.

Ultimately, however, high stall rates could simply indicate that the disk I/O subsystem is inadequate to handle the required I/O throughput. If attempts to reduce the overall I/O load fail to bring the stall rates down to acceptable levels, then there is little choice but to consider adding more or faster disks, more or faster I/O paths, or to investigate potential problems with the configuration of the I/O subsystem.

Finally, remember that the data in this DMV reflects only SQL Server's perspective of disk I/O. If the disk subsystem is shared at a server level with other applications, another application may be the actual cause of poor disk performance, not SQL Server. Furthermore, with use of SANs, virtualization software, and so on, there are often several "intermediary" layers between SQL Server and the actual disk storage.

In short, analyze carefully the data obtained from this DMV, and consider it in conjunction with data obtained from Windows OS counters, Profiler, and other DMVs, before deciding on a course of action.

Using sys.dm_os_performance_counters

Generally, it's probably easiest to collect performance counters using Performance Monitor (Perfmon), as discussed previously. However, if you prefer to save the statistics in a database table and interrogate them using SQL, the `sys.dm_os_performance_counters` DMV is a very useful tool. Just write the query to retrieve the data from the DMV, add `INSERT INTO CounterTrendingTableName…` and you have a rudimentary monitoring system! In addition, it's not always possible to get direct access to Perfmon, and accessing it from a different machine can be slow.

Unfortunately, using this DMV is far from plain sailing and a full description of its intricacies is out of scope here. Instead, we refer you to the book, *Performance Tuning with SQL Server Dynamic Management Views* (HTTP://WWW.SIMPLE-TALK.COM/BOOKS/ SQL-BOOKS/PERFORMANCE-TUNING-WITH-SQL-SERVER-DYNAMIC-MANAGEMENT-VIEWS/), which is available as a free eBook.

Listing 9.6, below, simply provides an example of how to report on log growth or shrink events. The output indicates that the **Persons** database (initial log size 2 MB, auto-growth increment 2 MB) underwent a huge number of log growth events, due to inserting the initial load of 1 million rows and then performing the update in Listing 9.2.

This is obviously a cause for concern and the DBA would need to investigate the log sizing and growth settings, and possibly perform a one-off shrink followed by appropriate resize, as described in Chapter 8.

```
DECLARE @object_name SYSNAME
SET @object_name = CASE WHEN @@servicename = 'MSSQLSERVER' THEN 'SQLServer'
                       ELSE 'MSSQL$' + @@serviceName
                  END + ':Databases'

DECLARE @PERF_COUNTER_LARGE_RAWCOUNT INT
SELECT  @PERF_COUNTER_LARGE_RAWCOUNT = 65792

SELECT  object_name ,
        counter_name ,
        instance_name ,
        cntr_value
FROM    sys.dm_os_performance_counters
WHERE   cntr_type = @PERF_COUNTER_LARGE_RAWCOUNT
        AND object_name = @object_name
        AND counter_name IN ( 'Log Growths', 'Log Shrinks' )
        AND cntr_value > 0
ORDER BY object_name ,
        counter_name ,
        instance_name
```

	object_name	counter_name	instance_name	cntr_value
1	SQLServer:Databases	Log Growths	_Total	4215
2	SQLServer:Databases	Log Growths	Persons	4017
3	SQLServer:Databases	Log Growths	Personslots	197
4	SQLServer:Databases	Log Growths	tempdb	1

Listing 9.6: Capturing log growth and shrink events.

T-SQL and PowerShell Scripting

There are several scripting approaches to monitoring all of your SQL Server instances for the size and properties of your database files, among many other things. This section doesn't attempt to cover all of the possible ways to collect this information, just to review the best ones of which we're aware.

T-SQL and SSIS

In his book, *SQL Server Tacklebox* (HTTP://WWW.SIMPLE-TALK.COM/BOOKS/SQL-BOOKS/ SQL-SERVER-TACKLEBOX/) Rodney Landrum provides T-SQL scripts to collect all manner of server and database information, including log and data file growth:

- **Server Information** – Server name, SQL Server version, collation information, and so on.

- **Database Management** – Primarily to monitor data and log file growth.

- **Database Backups** – Have backups run successfully? Which databases are in `FULL` recovery model versus `SIMPLE` or `BULK_LOGGED`? Are we doing regular log backups of `FULL` recovery databases?

- **Security** – Who has access to do what?

- **SQL Agent Jobs** – These could include those that run your database backups.

He then demonstrates how to automate the collection of this information, across all servers, using SSIS, and store it in a central DBA Repository database, for review and analysis.

If this sounds like the right approach for you, download the free eBook, and accompanying code, and try it out.

PowerShell

PowerShell, with Server Management Objects, forms a powerful automation tool for managing and documenting SQL Server databases. It's a rather steep learning curve for any DBA brought up on T-SQL and GUI management tools, but a few short scripts can gather all manner of data across all your servers, and all SQL Server versions.

The following two scripts are adapted from the work of PowerShell enthusiast Phil Factor; see HTTP://WWW.SIMPLE-TALK.COM/SQL/DATABASE-ADMINISTRATION/ POWERSHELL-SMO-JUST-WRITING-THINGS-ONCE/

The PowerShell routine in Listing 9.7 takes a list of SQL server instance names and checks all the databases within those server instances, listing out, via SMO:

- name of the log file and the path
- auto-growth setting (either KB or percent)
- current file size (MB), amount of space used (MB) and maximum file size (MB)
- number of disk reads, number of disk writes
- bytes read from disk and bytes written to disk.

Simply update the script with your server name and run it from Windows PowerShell.

```
#Load SMO assemblies
$MS='Microsoft.SQLServer'
@('.SMO') |
    foreach-object {
        if ([System.Reflection.Assembly]::LoadWithPartialName("$MS$_") -eq $null)
            {"missing SMO component $MS$_"}
    }
set-psdebug -strict
$ErrorActionPreference = "stop" # you can opt to stagger on, bleeding
                                # if an error occurs


$My="$MS.Management.Smo"
@("YourServerPath\InstanceName","MySecondServer") |
   foreach-object {new-object ("$My.Server") $_ } | # create an SMO server object
    Where-Object {$_.ServerType -ne $null} | # did you positively get the server?
     Foreach-object {$_.Databases } | #for every server successfully reached
      Where-Object {$_.IsSystemObject -ne $true} | #not the system objects
        foreach-object{$_.Logfiles} |
          Select-object @{Name="Server"; Expression={$_.parent.parent.name}},
                        @{Name="Database"; Expression={$_.parent.name}},
                        Name, Filename,
                        @{Name="Growth"; Expression={"$($_.Growth)
                                                    $($_.GrowthType)"}},
                        @{Name="size(mb)"; Expression={"{0:n2}" —f
                                                    ($_.size/1MB)}},
                        @{Name="MaxSize(mb)"; Expression={"{0:n2}" —f
                                                    ($_.MaxSize/1MB)}},
                        NumberOfDiskReads,NumberOfDiskWrites,
                        BytesReadFromDisk,BytesWrittenToDisk |
                Out-GridView
```

S..	Database	Name	FileName	Growth	size(mb)	MaxSize(mb)	NumberOf...	NumberOfDiskWrites	BytesReadFromDisk	BytesWritten
t...	Persons2012	Persons2012_log	D:\SQLData\Persons2012_log.ldf	2048 ...	0.36	2,048.00	748	4,344	3,968,000	165,981,184
t...	PersonsLots	PersonsLots_log	D:\SQLData\PersonsLots_log.ldf	2048 ...	2.04	2,048.00	4,177	46,389	18,017,792	1,996,482,04

Listing 9.7: Using PowerShell and SMO to investigate log file size, location and activity.

We've displayed the output in the grid view, and filtered to show only databases with the term "persons" in their name. If you'd prefer to output to Excel, simply replace `Out-GridView` with the following:

```
Convertto-csv —useculture > Export.csv
```

If you want run the script from within SSMS, right-click on the server or database and select **Start PowerShell**. If you're using anything other than the SQL 2012 version, then you'll need to first download, import and install the `sqlps` module, in order to get access to the `Out-GridView` and `Convertto-csv` cmdlets. See Michael Sorens's article for more details: HTTP://WWW.SIMPLE-TALK.COM/SQL/DATABASE-ADMINISTRATION/PRACTICAL-POWERSHELL-FOR-SQL-SERVER-DEVELOPERS-AND-DBAS-%E2%80%93-PART-1/. Alternatively, simply replace the last line with `FormatTable`.

Listing 9.8 shows a second routine, concerned with investigating log file fragmentation. Again, the routine uses SMO to query each database on all specified SQL Server instances. It queries `DBCC LogInfo`, via T-SQL, to get the number of VLFs for each log file. It groups the results to report the number of virtual log files, the size of the biggest VLF in MB, the smallest VLF in MB, and average and total size across all VLFs, for each database. This time, we use `FormatTable` for the output.

```
#Load SMO assemblies
$MS='Microsoft.SQLServer'
@('.SMO') |
    foreach-object {
        if ([System.Reflection.Assembly]::LoadWithPartialName("$MS$_") -eq $null)
            {"missing SMO component $MS$_"}
    }
set-psdebug -strict
$ErrorActionPreference = "stop" #

$My="$MS.Management.Smo" #
@("YourServerPath\InstanceName","MySecondServer") |
    foreach-object {new-object ("$My.Server") $_ } | # create an SMO server object
    Where-Object {$_.ServerType -ne $null} | # did you positively get the server?
      Foreach-object {$_.Databases } | #for every server successfully reached
          Foreach-object { #at this point you have reached the database
          $Db=$_
          $_.ExecuteWithResults('dbcc loginfo').Tables[0] | #make the DBCC query
            Measure-Object -minimum -maximum -average -sum FileSize |
                                                #group the results by filesize
              Select-object @{Name="Server"; Expression={$Db.parent.name}},
                        @{Name="Database"; Expression={$Db.name}},
                        @{Name="No.VLFs"; Expression={$_.Count}},
                        @{Name="MaxVLFSize(mb)"; Expression={"{0:n2}" -f
                                                ($_.Maximum/1MB)}},
                        @{Name="MinVLFSize(mb)"; Expression={"{0:n2}" -f
                                                ($_.Minimum/1MB)}},
                        @{Name="AverageVLF(mb)"; Expression={"{0:n2}" -f
                                                ($_.Average/1MB)}},
                        @{Name="SumVLF(mb)"; Expression={"{0:n2}" -f
                                                ($_.Sum/1MB)}}
                        } | Format-Table * -AutoSize
```

Database	No.VLFs	MaxVLFSize(mb)	MinVLFSize(mb)	AverageVLF(mb)	SumVLF(mb)
AdventureWorks2012	2	0.24	0.24	0.24	0.48
master	7	0.25	0.24	0.25	1.74
model	4	0.25	0.24	0.25	0.99
msdb	16	0.44	0.24	0.28	4.55
NewTest	4	0.26	0.25	0.25	1.01
Persons2012	744	0.68	0.44	0.50	371.99
PersonsLots	4172	0.68	0.44	0.50	2,085.99
tempdb	3	0.25	0.24	0.25	0.74
TestDB2012	4	0.68	0.44	0.50	1.99

Listing 9.8: Investigating log fragmentation with PowerShell and SMO (server name omitted from output).

Summary

This final chapter reviewed just a few of the tools available to the DBA for monitoring log growth and performance, including Windows Perfmon, third-party monitoring tools, Dynamic Management Views, and PowerShell or T-SQL scripting. We tried to offer a reasonable feel for what each tool can do, so that you can explore further if it looks like a good fit for your needs.

It is essential that every DBA maintains a healthy transaction log. Ideally, this will consist of a single log file, on a dedicated RAID 1+0 array (or as close to this ideal as you can get) in order to support maximum write performance and throughput. We must capture "baseline" statistics that characterize log write performance under typical workload, and then monitor this data over time, checking for abnormal activity, or sudden deterioration in performance.

Likewise, we should also size in accordance with the current and predicted data load, rather than let SQL Server "manage" log growth via auto-growth events. We should enable SQL Server's auto-growth facility but only as a safeguard, and the DBA should receive an alert when log growth occurs, and investigate. By carefully monitoring log growth, we can avoid situations such as a full transaction log, or a highly fragmented log, which might impede performance of operations that read the log, such as log backups and the crash recovery process.

Further Reading

- **Storage Testing and Monitoring (video)**
  HTTP://TECHNET.MICROSOFT.COM/EN-US/SQLSERVER/GG508910.ASPX

- **Baselining and Benchmarking (video)**
  HTTP://TECHNET.MICROSOFT.COM/EN-US/SQLSERVER/GG429821.ASPX

- **Back to Basics: Capturing Baselines on Production SQL Servers**
  HTTP://WWW.SQLSERVERCENTRAL.COM/ARTICLES/BASELINES/94656/

- **Diagnosing Transaction Log Performance Issues and Limits of the Log Manager**
  HTTP://SQLCAT.COM/SQLCAT/B/TECHNICALNOTES/ARCHIVE/2008/12/09/DIAGNOSING-
  TRANSACTION-LOG-PERFORMANCE-ISSUES-AND-LIMITS-OF-THE-LOG-MANAGER.ASPX

- **Monitoring SQL Server Virtual Log File Fragmentation**
  HTTP://WWW.SIMPLE-TALK.COM/SQL/DATABASE-ADMINISTRATION/
  MONITORING-SQL-SERVER-VIRTUAL-LOG-FILE-FRAGMENTATION/

- **Monitoring SQL Server database transaction log space**
  HTTP://WWW.MSSQLTIPS.COM/SQLSERVERTIP/1178/
  MONITORING-SQL-SERVER-DATABASE-TRANSACTION-LOG-SPACE/

- **System Data Collection Sets**
  HTTP://MSDN.MICROSOFT.COM/EN-US/LIBRARY/BB964725%28V=SQL.100%29.ASPX

- **The Future – fn_dblog() No More? Tracking Transaction Log Activity in Denali**
  HTTP://WWW.SQLSKILLS.COM/BLOGS/JONATHAN/POST/AN-XEVENT-A-DAY-(22-OF-31)-
  E28093-THE-FUTURE-E28093-FN_DBLOG()-NO-MORE-TRACKING-TRANSACTION-LOG-
  ACTIVITY-IN-DENALI.ASPX

Acknowledgements

We would like to thank:

- Louis Davidson, who, in the *Dynamic Management Objects* section of
  this chapter, allowed us to reproduce material from his book, which he
  co-authored with Tim Ford: *Performance Tuning with SQL Server Dynamic
  Management Views* (HTTP://WWW.SIMPLE-TALK.COM/BOOKS/SQL-BOOKS/
  PERFORMANCE-TUNING-WITH-SQL-SERVER-DYNAMIC-MANAGEMENT-VIEWS/)

- Phil Factor for his help with the PowerShell script.

Index

A

ACID properties (atomicity, consistency, isolation, durability) 17
ACTIVE_BACKUP_OR_RESTORE 144
Active log 27–30
Active transactions 133–142
    identifying 138–142
    long-running transactions 134–137
    uncommitted transactions 137–138
ALTER INDEX REBUILD 123
ALTER INDEX REORGANIZE 124
Architecture. *See* Log architecture; *See also* Physical architecture
Auto-growth. *See* Log growth
Auto-truncate mode 50, 60, 65

B

Backup set 69
Backupset table 65
Backups (log) 43–45
    automating 57–58
    choosing what type 45–47
    differential 44
    file and filegroup 45
    frequency 54–55
    full 44, 50
    logistics 54–58
    storing 56
    tail log. *See* Log backups
    third-party tools 58
    transaction 44
    verifying 57–58

bcp 49, 90, 99
Bulk load 91
BULK_LOGGED recovery model 89–118
    advantages of 98–102
    best practices 115–117
    minimally logged operations 90–102

C

Checkpoint process 17, 60
Compensation log records 39, 181
Controlling excessive logging 125–127
COPY_ONLY log backup 21
Crash recovery process (restart recovery) 11, 17, 103–104, 166, 173, 180
CreateLSN 36

D

DATABASE_MIRRORING 145–146
Data purging 134
DBCC DBREINDEX (deprecated) 123
DBCC INDEXDEFRAG (deprecated) 124
DBCC LogInfo 35
DBCC SHRINKFILE 185
DBCC SQLPERF (LOGSPACE) 22
Differential Changed Map 93
Dynamic Management Views and Functions (DMVs) 197–204
    sys.dm_db_log_space_usage 198
    sys.dm_io_pending_io_requests 197
    sys.dm_io_virtual_file_stats 197, 198–202
    sys.dm_os_performance_counters 203–204

E

Error 9002. *See* **Transaction log full (9002) error**

F

fn_dblog 84, 93
fn_dump_dblog 84, 93
FSeqNo 36
FULL recovery model 63–88
    without log backups 131–133

G

Global Allocation Maps (GAMs) 96

H

Hardware 155–179
Heavy log-writing transactions 127–129

I

Index 122
    Allocation Maps (IAMs) 96
    maintenance operations 122
        excessive logging 122–129
        rebuilds 123–124
        reorganization 124–125
INSERT INTO...SELECT 99
Instant file initialization 121
IOmeter 164

L

Lack of log space reuse 130–142
last_log_backup_lsn 53
Lazy Writer 17

Log architecture 156
Log backups. *See also* **Backups (log)**
    basics 64–68
        interrogate backupset table 64–65
    methods of 65–66
    restore. *See* Restore and recovery
    tail log backups 66–68
        when the database is offline 85–86
Log chain 55–56
    breaking 56
Log fragmentation 41, 164–179
    effect on crash recovery 173–179
    effect on log backups 167–173
Log growth 33–41, 142. *See also* **Active transactions**; *See also* **FULL recovery model: without log backups**; *See also* **Lack of log space reuse**; *See also* **Pending replication**
    excessive 119–154
    proper management 152
Logical Sequence Number (LSN) 28. *See also* **MaxLSN (head of the log)**; *See also* **MinLSN (tail of the log)**
    LSN-based restore 85
    LSN chain 28
Log internal processes 27–42
Log record 15
Log reservation 39
Log sizing 180–182
Log throughput
    optimizing 155–188
Log truncation. *See* **Truncation**

M

Marked transactions 78

MaxLSN (head of the log) 29

Minimal logging 49, 63, 68

    advantages of 98–102

    and crash recovery 103–104

    and database restores 104–107

    and log backup size 108–109

    and tail log backups 109–115

    implications of 102–115

    versus "extent de-allocation only" 97

MinLSN (tail of the log) 28

Mismanagement 119, 149–152

    detach database, delete log file 149–150

    force log file truncation 150–151

    scheduled shrinking of the transaction log 151–152

Model database 23

Monitoring tools 190–196

O

Offline database backups. See Log backups: tail log backups

Online index rebuild 123

P

Page Free Space (PFS) 93

Pending replication. See Truncation: factors that delay

Perfmon. See Windows Performance Monitor

Physical architecture 155–179

    dedicated drive/array 161–162

Point-in-time restore. See Restore and recovery

PowerShell/SMO scripting 58, 205–209

Pseudo-SIMPLE recovery model 50

R

RAID (Redundant Array of Independent Disks) 162

    RAID level, choosing 162–179

Random I/O 161

Recovery models 47–54

    BULK_LOGGED 48. See also BULK_LOGGED recovery model

    choosing 48–49

    discovering 50–53

    FULL 48. See also FULL recovery model

    setting 49

    SIMPLE 47. See also SIMPLE recovery model

    switching 53–54

Recovery Point Objective (RPO) 132

Red Gate SQL Monitor 189, 196

Redo 173–177. See also Roll forward (redo) process

Remedial actions 183–187

Restore and recovery 68–86

    full restore to point of failure 69–71

    point-in-time restores 77–85

        to a marked transaction 78–81

        to a standby database 81–85

    restore to end of log backup 72–77

RESTORE...WITH...NORECOVERY 67

RESTORE...WITH...NO_TRUNCATE 67

RESTORE...WITH...RECOVERY 68

RESTORE...WITH...REPLACE 75

RESTORE...WITH...STANDBY 77

RESTORE...WITH...STOPAT 83

RESTORE...WITH...STOPBEFOREMARK 77

Roll back (undo) process 18, 39, 178-179

Roll forward (redo) process 17, 48, 83, 173-177

S

Scripts 13, 24, 57, 70, 126

SELECT...INTO 91, 92, 99

Sequential file 27

Sequential I/O 161

Server Management Objects. *See* PowerShell/SMO scripting

Service Level Agreement (SLA) 43, 89, 115

Shrinking the log 151-154, 185

SIMPLE recovery model

    limitations and advantages 61

    log management 59-61

SQLIO 164

    SQLIOSim 164

SQL Server

    benchmarking storage configurations 164

SSMS Maintenance Plans Wizard and Designer 57

T

Tail log backups 109-115. *See also* Log backups

Thread statics. *See* Statics

Transactional consistency 16-18

Transaction log 15-26

    and SQL Server 15-16

    backup and restore 18-19, 43-58

        backup example 22-25

    controlling the size of 20-25

    monitoring 189-212

    number of VLFs 166

    operations reading 166

    processes. *See* Log internal processes

Transaction log full (9002) error 32, 146-148

Truncation 21, 31-33

    and database recovery models 20

    and VLFs 31

    factors that delay 33, 130

T-SQL scripts 57

    T_SQL and SSIS 205

U

Uncontrolled growth of the transaction log 121-146

Undo. *See* Roll back (undo) process

V

Virtual Log File (VLF) 20, 27-30

    transaction log VLFs 120

W

Windows Performance Monitor (Perfmon) 189, 190-195

WITH NO_TRUNCATE 85

Write ahead logging 16-18

X

XACT_ABORT 18

SQL Server
and .NET Tools
from Red Gate Software

Pricing and information about Red Gate tools are correct at the time of
going to print. For the latest information and pricing on all Red Gate's
tools, visit www.red-gate.com

ingeniously simple tools

SQL Compare® Pro $595

Compare and synchronize SQL Server database schemas

→ Eliminate mistakes migrating database changes from dev, to test, to production
→ Speed up the deployment of new database schema updates
→ Find and fix errors caused by differences between databases
→ Compare and synchronize within SSMS

> **"Just purchased SQL Compare. With the productivity I'll get out of this tool, it's like buying time."**
> **Robert Sondles** Blueberry Island Media Ltd

SQL Data Compare Pro $595

Compares and synchronizes SQL Server

→ Save time by automatically comparing and synchronizing your data
→ Copy lookup data from development databases to staging or production
→ Quickly fix problems by restoring damaged or missing data to a single row
→ Compare and synchronize data within SSMS

> **"We use SQL Data Compare daily and it has become an indispensable part of delivering our service to our customers. It has also streamlined our daily update process and cut back literally a good solid hour per day."**
> **George Pantela** GPAnalysis.com

Visit **www.red-gate.com** for a 14-day, free trial

SQL Prompt Pro

$295

Write, edit, and explore SQL effortlessly

- → Write SQL smoothly, with code-completion and SQL snippets
- → Reformat SQL to a preferred style
- → Keep databases tidy by finding invalid objects automatically
- → Save time and effort with script summaries, smart object renaming, and more

> "SQL Prompt is hands-down one of the coolest applications I've used. Makes querying/developing so much easier and faster."
>
> **Jorge Segarra** University Community Hospital

SQL Source Control

from **$395**

Connect your existing source control system to SQL Server

- → Bring all the benefits of source control to your database
- → Source control database schemas and data within SSMS, not with offline scripts
- → Connect your databases to TFS, SVN, SourceGear Vault, Vault Pro, Mercurial, Perforce, Git, Bazaar, and any source control system with a capable command line
- → Work with shared development databases, or individual copies
- → Track changes to follow who changed what, when, and why
- → Keep teams in sync with easy access to the latest database version
- → View database development history for easy retrieval of specific versions

Visit **www.red-gate.com** for a free trial

 **Deployment Manager**   from **$295**

Automated deployment for your applications and databases

→ Deploys your whole application – ASP.NET sites, dependent assemblies, and databases – in one process

→ Makes deployment repeatable with a minimum of custom scripting

→ Shows you which version of your software is running on each dev, test, staging, and production environment, from a central dashboard

→ Works with local, remote, and Cloud-based servers

→ Uses public/private key encryption to keep deployments over the Internet secure

"This tool ranks up there with NuGet and Team City as the tools that have made the biggest difference to web application development productivity these last months – it truly deserves to be a roaring success!"
Mark Roberts
.NET Web Developer, Red Gate Software

Visit **www.red-gate.com** for a 28-day, free trial

SQL Backup Pro

$795

Compress, verify, and encrypt SQL Server backups

➔ Compress SQL Server database backups by up to 95% for faster, smaller backups

➔ Protect your data with up to 256-bit AES encryption

➔ Strengthen your backups with network resilience to enable a fault-tolerant transfer of backups across flaky networks

➔ Control your backup activities through an intuitive interface, with powerful job management and an interactive timeline

➔ Get integrated backup verification – schedule regular restores and include a database integrity check (DBCC CHECKDB)

"SQL Backup Pro cut the backup time for our most mission-critical database by 92%, and provided us with 95% compression. Built-in network resilience has also reduced our failure rate to zero. I'm absolutely amazed at how well it performs."

Kiara Rodemaker
Manager, IT Accounting Services, Czarnowski

Visit **www.red-gate.com** for a 14-day, free trial

 **SQL Monitor**   from **$795**

SQL Server performance monitoring and alerting

→ Intuitive overviews at global, cluster, machine, SQL Server, and database levels for up-to-the-minute performance data

→ Use SQL Monitor's web UI to keep an eye on server performance in real time on desktop machines and mobile devices

→ Intelligent SQL Server alerts via email and an alert inbox in the UI, so you know about problems first

→ Comprehensive historical data, so you can go back in time to identify the source of a problem

→ View the top 10 expensive queries for an instance or database based on CPU usage, duration, and reads and writes

→ PagerDuty integration for phone and SMS alerting

→ Fast, simple installation and administration

→ Add your own T-SQL scripts with the custom metrics feature to expand SQL Monitor's range

> **"Being web based, SQL Monitor is readily available to you, wherever you may be on your network. You can check on your servers from almost any location, via most mobile devices that support a web browser."**
>
> **Jonathan Allen**
> Senior DBA, Careers South West Ltd

Visit **www.red-gate.com** for a 14-day, free trial

SQL DBA Bundle $1,395

Five essential tools for database administration

Backup & Recovery

Protect your organization's data by creating highly compressed, fully verified and encrypted backups, and ensure reliable restores.

Performance Monitoring & Tuning

Monitor your servers in real time and obtain the performance data and alerts that are important to your business.

Storage & Capacity Planning

Proactively monitor data growth and make the most of your storage space with backup compression and the ability to virtually restore.

Troubleshooting

Get an alert within seconds of a problem arising, gain insight into what happened, and diagnose the issue, fast.

Security

Protect your data from unauthorized access with strong backup encryption.

The SQL DBA Bundle contains:

SQL Backup Pro   SQL Monitor   SQL Virtual Restore   SQL HyperBac   SQL Multi Script

The tools in the bundle can be bought separately with a combined value of $3,375, or purchased together for **$1,395, saving 60% on the individual tool prices.**

Visit **www.red-gate.com** for a 14-day, free trial

SQL Toolbelt $1,995

The essential SQL Server tools for database professionals

You can buy our acclaimed SQL Server tools individually or bundled. Our most popular deal is the SQL Toolbelt: sixteen of our SQL Server tools in a single installer, with a combined value of $5,930 but an actual price of **$1,995, a saving of 66%**.

Fully compatible with SQL Server 2000, 2005, and 2008.

SQL Toolbelt contains:

→ **SQL Compare Pro**

→ **SQL Data Compare Pro**

→ **SQL Source Control**

→ **SQL Backup Pro**

→ **SQL Monitor**

→ **SQL Prompt Pro**

→ **SQL Data Generator**

→ **SQL Doc**

→ **SQL Test**

→ **SQL Dependency Tracker**

→ **SQL Packager**

→ **SQL Multi Script Unlimited**

→ **SQL Search**

→ **SQL Comparison SDK**

→ **SQL Object Level Recovery Native**

→ **SQL Connect**

"The SQL Toolbelt provides tools that database developers, as well as DBAs, should not live without."
William Van Orden Senior Database Developer, Lockheed Martin

Visit **www.red-gate.com** for a 14-day, free trial

ANTS Memory Profiler $495

Find memory leaks and optimize memory usage of your .NET applications

→ Zero in on the causes of memory leaks, fast

→ Visualize the relationship between your objects and identify references which should no longer be held in memory

→ Optimize your application's memory usage

> "Freaking sweet! We have a known memory leak that took me about four hours to find using our current tool, so I fired up ANTS Memory Profiler and went at it like I didn't know the leak existed. Not only did I come to the conclusion much faster, but I found another one!"
>
> **Aaron Smith** IT Manager, R.C. Systems Inc.

ANTS Performance Profiler from $495

Identify performance bottlenecks within minutes

→ Drill down to slow lines of code with line-level code timings

→ Analyse both your .NET code and SQL queries in a single profiling session

→ Optimize .NET application performance

> "ANTS Performance Profiler took us straight to the specific areas of our code which were the cause of our performance issues."
>
> **Terry Phillips** Sr Developer, Harley-Davidson Dealer Systems

> "I have integrated ANTS Profiler into my entire development process and it has truly helped us write better performing applications from the beginning by ensuring that we always know exactly what is going on."
>
> **Mitchell Sellers** MVP

Visit **www.red-gate.com** for a 14-day, free trial

.NET Reflector

$95

"EVERY DEVELOPER NEEDS THIS TOOL!"
Daniel Larson Software Architect, NewsGator Technologies

Decompile, debug, and understand any .NET code

→ See inside assemblies, libraries, and frameworks so you can understand how they work, even if you don't have the source

→ Decompile, search, and analyze any .NET assembly in C#, Visual Basic, and IL

→ Step straight into decompiled assemblies while debugging in Visual Studio, so you can debug 3rd-party code just like your own

"One of the most useful, practical debugging tools that I have ever worked with in .NET! It provides complete browsing and debugging features for .NET assemblies, and has clean integration with Visual Studio."
Tom Baker Consultant Software Engineer, EMC Corporation

SmartAssembly

$795

Prepare your application for the world

→ Obfuscation: Obfuscate your .NET code to secure it against reverse engineering. Multiple layers of protection defend your software against decompilation and cracking.

→ Automated Error Reporting: Get quick and automatic reports on exceptions your end-users encounter, and identify unforeseen bugs within hours or days of shipping. Receive detailed reports containing a stack trace and values of the local variables, making debugging easier.

"Knowing the frequency of problems (especially immediately after a release) is extremely helpful in prioritizing and triaging bugs that are reported internally. Additionally, by having the context of where those errors occurred, including debugging information, really gives you that leap forward to start troubleshooting and diagnosing the issue."
Ed Blankenship
Technical Lead and MVP

Visit **www.red-gate.com** for a 14-day, free trial

SQL Server Execution Plans (2nd Edition)
Grant Fritchey

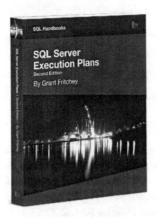

Every Database Administrator, developer, report writer, and anyone else who writes T-SQL to access SQL Server data, must understand how to read and interpret execution plans. This book leads you right from the basics of capturing plans, through to how to interpret them in their various forms, graphical or XML, and then how to use the information you find there to diagnose the most common causes of poor query performance, and so optimize your SQL queries, and improve your indexing strategy.

ISBN: 978-1-906434-93-9
Published: October 2012

SQL Server Concurrency:
Locking, Blocking and Row Versioning
Kalen Delaney

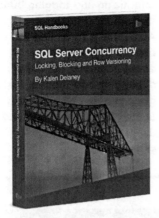

Your application can have impeachable indexes and queries, but they won't help you if you can't get to your data because another application has it locked. That's why every DBA and developer must understand SQL Server concurrency and how to troubleshoot excessive blocking or deadlocking.

ISBN: 978-1-906434-91-5
Published: September 2012

The Red Gate Guides

SQL Server Backup and Restore

Shawn McGehee

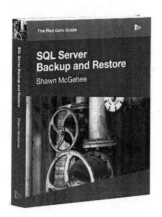

A DBA's tasks from day to day are rarely constant; with one exception: the need to ensure each and every day that any database in their charge can be restored and recovered, in the event of error or disaster. In this book, you'll discover how to perform each of these backup and restore operations using SQL Server Management Studio (SSMS), basic T-SQL scripts and Red Gate's SQL Backup tool.

ISBN: 978-1-906434-86-1
Published: May 2012

SQL Server Team-based Development

Phil Factor, Grant Fritchey, Alex Kuznetsov, and Mladen Prajdić

This book shows how to use a mixture of home-grown scripts, native SQL Server tools, and tools from the Red Gate SQL Toolbelt, to successfully develop database applications in a team environment, and make database development as similar as possible to "normal" development.

ISBN: 978-1-906434-59-5
Published: November 2010

Lightning Source UK Ltd.
Milton Keynes UK
UKOW011434100613

212035UK00003B/116/P